GO IDIOMS AND BEST PRACTICES
FOR DEVELOPERS

Mastering the Language of Code: Essential Idioms and
Best Practices for Developers

SIMON TELLIER

TABLE OF CONTENTS

Chapter 1: Introduction to Go and Idiomatic Programming

1.1 Why Go? The Philosophy Behind the Language

Go, often referred to as Golang, was born from a desire to simplify software development while maintaining efficiency and scalability. Created by a team at Google in 2007—Robert Griesemer, Rob Pike, and Ken Thompson—Go was officially released as an open-source project in 2009. Its design reflects years of experience and frustration with existing languages, making it a breath of fresh air for modern developers.

At its core, Go prioritizes simplicity, readability, and performance. The creators of Go were driven by the challenges they faced at Google: managing massive codebases, maintaining high performance across distributed systems, and ensuring developer productivity. Traditional languages like C++ and Java, while powerful, often came with steep learning curves and overly complex toolchains. Go was designed to tackle these pain points head-on.

The philosophy of Go revolves around three key pillars:

1. **Simplicity and Readability**
   Go's syntax is clean and concise, making it easy to read and write. Unlike other languages, where cleverness or verbosity might take precedence, Go encourages straightforward code. The focus on simplicity ensures that even large teams working on complex systems can collaborate effectively. This makes Go particularly appealing for enterprise-grade applications, where code maintainability is as crucial as performance.

2. **Concurrency as a First-Class Citizen**
   In a world where distributed computing and multicore processors dominate, Go stands out for its concurrency model. Goroutines—lightweight threads managed by Go's runtime—allow developers to build scalable systems without the

complexities of traditional threading. Combined with channels, which enable safe communication between goroutines, Go simplifies concurrent programming in a way that few other languages can match.

3. **Fast Compilation and Execution**

   Go was built to compile quickly, even for large projects. Its single-binary outputs eliminate the dependency hell common in other ecosystems. As a compiled language, it offers near-C-level performance while maintaining the developer-friendly aspects of higher-level languages.

Other notable features of Go include:

- **Garbage Collection**: Automates memory management without sacrificing speed.
- **Cross-Platform Compatibility**: Go binaries can run seamlessly across different operating systems.
- **Standard Library**: Packed with utilities for networking, file handling, testing, and more, Go reduces reliance on third-party packages.

In short, Go was designed to meet the demands of modern software development: high performance, scalability, and developer productivity. Its philosophy emphasizes writing code that is clear, maintainable, and efficient.

1.2 Understanding Idiomatic Programming in Go

Idiomatic programming refers to writing code that adheres to the conventions and best practices of a given language. In Go, idiomatic code not only ensures consistency across projects but also maximizes the strengths of the language itself. While you *can* write Go code that looks like C++ or Python, you'll often miss out on the elegance and efficiency that idiomatic Go offers.

What Does Idiomatic Go Look Like?

Idiomatic Go is characterized by simplicity, readability, and adherence to Go's philosophy. Some key traits include:

- Minimalistic and clean syntax.
- Avoiding unnecessary abstractions.
- Favoring composition over inheritance.
- Emphasizing clear error handling over exceptions.
- Using goroutines and channels to simplify concurrency.

For example, Go avoids verbose error messages and complex exception hierarchies in favor of a simple pattern:

go

Copy

```
if err != nil {

    return err

}
```

This approach, while repetitive, is deliberate. It makes errors explicit and encourages developers to address them immediately rather than relying on hidden mechanisms.

Why Is Idiomatic Go Important?

1. **Improved Collaboration**: Following idiomatic practices ensures that teams can quickly understand and work on each other's code. This is especially crucial for open-source projects or large teams.
2. **Leveraging Go's Strengths**: By sticking to Go's conventions, developers can write code that's optimized for the language's runtime and tools.

3. **Code Maintainability**: Clean, idiomatic code is easier to maintain and extend over time.

Core Concepts in Idiomatic Go

1. **The Zero Value**

   Go's "zero value" philosophy ensures that variables have a predictable default state. For instance:
   - Integers default to 0.
   - Strings default to "".
   - Booleans default to false.
   - Slices, maps, and pointers default to nil.
2. This eliminates uninitialized variables and reduces runtime errors.

Interfaces Instead of Inheritance

Go favors interfaces over complex inheritance hierarchies. Interfaces in Go are implicit, meaning a type automatically satisfies an interface if it implements the required methods. This encourages decoupled, modular code.

Example:

go

Copy

```go
type Speaker interface {

   Speak() string

}

type Dog struct{}

func (d Dog) Speak() string {

   return "Woof!"

}
```

```go
func main() {

    var s Speaker = Dog{}

    fmt.Println(s.Speak())

}
```

3. In this example, Dog implements the Speaker interface without explicitly declaring it. This makes Go's interface system both flexible and powerful.

Composition Over Inheritance

Go encourages struct embedding to achieve functionality sharing instead of relying on inheritance. This allows developers to create flexible, reusable components.

Example:

go

Copy

```go
type Animal struct {

    Name string

}

type Dog struct {

    Animal

}

func (d Dog) Speak() string {

    return d.Name + " says Woof!"

}
```

5

```go
func main() {

    d := Dog{Animal{Name: "Buddy"}}

    fmt.Println(d.Speak())

}
```

4. **Clear and Explicit Error Handling**

   Go's approach to errors prioritizes clarity and simplicity. Errors are treated as regular values, encouraging developers to address them immediately.

   Example:

   go

   Copy

```go
func divide(a, b int) (int, error) {

    if b == 0 {

        return 0, fmt.Errorf("cannot divide by zero")

    }

    return a / b, nil

}
```

5. **Concurrency With Goroutines and Channels**

   Go's concurrency model is one of its most defining features. Goroutines are lightweight and can be launched with minimal overhead, while channels provide a safe way to share data between them.

   Example:

   go

```
Copy
func main() {

ch := make(chan int)

go func() {

  ch <- 42

}()

fmt.Println(<-ch)

}
```

6. **Common Pitfalls to Avoid**

While writing idiomatic Go, it's important to avoid:

- Overcomplicating solutions with unnecessary abstractions.
- Using panic and recover for general error handling (they should be reserved for truly exceptional cases).
- Ignoring the benefits of Go's built-in tools like gofmt for code formatting.

Tools to Help Write Idiomatic Go

- gofmt: Automatically formats your code to match Go's style guide.
- golangci-lint: A powerful linter to catch non-idiomatic patterns.
- **Effective Go**: An official guide from the Go team that outlines best practices.

Idiomatic Go is more than just a coding style; it's a way of thinking that aligns with the language's core philosophy. By understanding and applying these principles, developers can write Go code that's not only efficient and maintainable but also a pleasure to read and work with.

1.3 Benefits of Writing Idiomatic Go Code

Writing idiomatic Go code isn't just about adhering to conventions—it's about leveraging the design of the language to create efficient, maintainable, and collaborative solutions. By embracing idiomatic practices, developers align with Go's philosophy and unlock a range of practical benefits.

1. Enhanced Readability

Idiomatic Go prioritizes simplicity and clarity. Code written in this style is easy to read, even for someone who didn't originally write it. This is particularly valuable for large teams or open-source projects where multiple developers contribute. With Go's clean syntax and predictable patterns, idiomatic code minimizes ambiguity and allows developers to quickly understand the intent behind the code.

For example, instead of crafting a convoluted abstraction, Go developers might favor a straightforward approach:

go

Copy

```go
// Idiomatic Go: Simple and clear

if err != nil {

    log.Fatalf("Error: %v", err)

}
```

This readability helps teams onboard new developers more quickly and reduces the time spent deciphering overly complex solutions.

---

2. Easier Maintenance

Codebases evolve over time, and maintaining a large project can become a nightmare if the code isn't consistent. Idiomatic Go ensures uniformity, making it easier to update, debug, or extend existing code. By following established practices, you reduce the chances of introducing technical debt or creating code that only "works" for one person.

Consider a scenario where a team revisits a project after six months. Non-idiomatic code might require hours of reverse-engineering, while idiomatic code allows developers to make changes confidently and efficiently.

---

3. Improved Collaboration

When a team agrees on idiomatic practices, they create a shared understanding of how Go code should look and behave. This eliminates unnecessary debates over stylistic preferences and allows everyone to focus on solving problems. Go's official tools, such as gofmt, help enforce a standard format across the board, ensuring that code looks consistent regardless of who writes it.

---

4. Leveraging Go's Tools Effectively

Go's ecosystem is built around its idioms. Tools like gofmt, golangci-lint, and go vet are designed to work seamlessly with idiomatic Go code. Writing non-idiomatic code can lead to unnecessary friction with these tools, potentially missing out on valuable features like automatic formatting, linting, and error detection.

For example, if you follow Go's idiomatic error-handling pattern, go vet can identify common mistakes or potential runtime issues.

---

5. Better Performance

Idiomatic Go code often results in better performance, as it aligns with the design of the Go runtime. For instance, Go's philosophy of "communicate by sharing memory" ensures that developers avoid unnecessary locking and data races. By embracing idiomatic concurrency patterns like goroutines and channels, developers can write highly scalable systems with minimal resource overhead.

---

6. Increased Adoption and Longevity

Idiomatic Go makes your codebase accessible to the broader Go community. This is especially important for open-source projects, where contributors expect a certain level of familiarity and adherence to conventions. A well-written, idiomatic codebase is more likely to attract contributors, gain adoption, and remain relevant in the long term.

---

7. Reduced Bugs and Errors

By adhering to Go's conventions, developers naturally avoid common pitfalls and anti-patterns. For instance, Go's explicit error-handling pattern encourages developers to address potential failures immediately, reducing the risk of unnoticed errors propagating through the system.

Example:

```go
Copy
// Idiomatic error handling
file, err := os.Open("config.json")
if err != nil {
    return fmt.Errorf("failed to open file: %w", err)
}
defer file.Close()
```

This proactive approach prevents unexpected behaviors and ensures robustness.

---

8. Community Recognition

Go's community places a strong emphasis on writing idiomatic code. Developers who follow these practices gain recognition and respect within the community, as their code reflects a deep understanding of the language. This can open doors to professional opportunities and collaborations.

1.4 Overview of the Go Ecosystem and Community

Go isn't just a programming language—it's a thriving ecosystem supported by an active and passionate community. From its standard library to open-source frameworks and tools, the Go ecosystem is designed to help developers build robust applications

11

efficiently. Let's explore the key components and resources that make Go a standout choice for developers.

The Go Standard Library

One of Go's biggest strengths is its robust standard library. It provides a rich set of built-in packages that cover a wide range of use cases, from file handling to networking. This reduces the need for external dependencies and allows developers to get started with powerful tools right out of the box.

Key features of the standard library:

- **Networking:** net/http for building web servers and handling HTTP requests.
- **Concurrency:** sync and context for managing goroutines and shared state.
- **File Handling:** os and io packages for working with files and input/output streams.
- **Testing:** testing for writing and running unit tests.

For example, you can build a simple web server using just the standard library:

go

Copy

```go
package main

import (

  "fmt"

  "net/http"

)
```

```go
func handler(w http.ResponseWriter, r *http.Request) {

    fmt.Fprintf(w, "Hello, World!")

}

func main() {

    http.HandleFunc("/", handler)

    http.ListenAndServe(":8080", nil)

}
```

Go Tools

The Go toolchain is designed to simplify development workflows. Some of the most popular tools include:

- **gofmt**: Automatically formats code to follow Go's style guidelines.
- **go mod**: Manages dependencies and modules.
- **go test**: Runs unit tests and benchmarks.
- **go vet**: Analyzes code for potential issues.

These tools are lightweight, fast, and integrated directly into the Go runtime.

Popular Frameworks and Libraries

While the standard library is extensive, the Go community has also developed a wide range of open-source frameworks and libraries. Some notable examples include:

13

- **Web Frameworks:** Gin, Echo, and Fiber for building APIs and web applications.
- **Database Libraries:** GORM and sqlx for working with relational databases.
- **CLI Tools:** Cobra for building command-line applications.
- **Concurrency Utilities:** Worker pools, task schedulers, and enhanced channel utilities.

Go's Open-Source Community

The Go community is one of the most active and welcoming in the programming world. Developers regularly contribute to open-source projects, share knowledge through blogs and conferences, and offer help on forums like Reddit and Stack Overflow.

Key community resources:

- **Go Forum:** A friendly space for developers to ask questions and share ideas.
- **Go Blog:** Official updates, tutorials, and insights from the Go team.
- **GitHub:** Countless open-source repositories for libraries, frameworks, and tools.

Conferences and Meetups

Go has a strong presence in the tech conference scene, with events like GopherCon drawing thousands of developers annually. These events are excellent opportunities to learn, network, and gain insights into the latest trends in Go development.

Staying Updated

The Go language is constantly evolving, with regular releases introducing new features and improvements. Developers can stay informed by:

- Following the official Go release notes.
- Subscribing to newsletters like Go Weekly.
- Joining communities on Slack or Discord.

The Go ecosystem and community provide everything developers need to build high-quality applications, from powerful tools to collaborative resources. Whether you're a solo developer or part of a large team, Go's ecosystem ensures you have the support and capabilities to succeed

Chapter 2: Essential Go Idioms

2.1 The "Zero Value" Principle and How It Simplifies Code

One of Go's most fundamental idioms is the "zero value" principle. Unlike many other programming languages, Go initializes variables with a default value when they are declared but not explicitly assigned. This principle not only eliminates uninitialized variables but also simplifies code and enhances reliability.

What Is the Zero Value?

The zero value is the default value assigned to a variable of a specific type when no value is explicitly provided. These defaults are predictable and consistent, making it easier to work with variables without worrying about their state.

Here are some examples of zero values for common types in Go:

- **Numeric types (int, float64)**: 0
- **Boolean**: false
- **String**: "" (empty string)
- **Pointers, slices, maps, channels, interfaces, and functions**: nil

Example:

go

Copy

```
package main

import "fmt"
```

```go
func main() {

    var i int      // Zero value is 0

    var b bool     // Zero value is false

    var s string   // Zero value is an empty string

    var p *int     // Zero value is nil

    fmt.Printf("i: %d, b: %t, s: '%s', p: %v\n", i, b, s, p)

}
```

Output:

yaml

Copy

i: 0, b: false, s: '', p: <nil>

Benefits of the Zero Value Principle

1. **No Uninitialized Variables** In languages where uninitialized variables hold arbitrary or garbage values, developers need to be extra cautious. Go eliminates this problem entirely by ensuring all variables have a well-defined initial state.

Simpler Code The zero value reduces the need for redundant initialization code. Developers don't need to explicitly assign default values to variables unless they differ from the zero value.
Example:

17

```go
type Config struct {

    Port    int

    Debug   bool

    Timeout float64

}

func main() {

    var cfg Config // All fields initialized to their zero values

    fmt.Printf("Config: %+v\n", cfg)

}
```

Output:
```css
Config: {Port:0 Debug:false Timeout:0}
```

2. **Fewer Runtime Errors** By initializing complex types like pointers and slices to nil, Go ensures that developers handle these states explicitly before using them, reducing the risk of undefined behavior.

Working With the Zero Value in Practice

Default Return Values Functions in Go return the zero value for all result variables if no explicit return value is provided.

18

Example:

go

Copy

```go
func getName() string {

    return // Implicitly returns "" (zero value for string)

}

func main() {

    fmt.Println(getName()) // Output: ""

}
```

1. **Nil Checks** When working with pointers, slices, maps, and channels, you can check for nil to determine whether they have been initialized.
   Example:
   go
   Copy

```go
var numbers []int // Zero value is nil

if numbers == nil {

    fmt.Println("The slice is nil!")

}
```

2. **Avoiding Overhead** Declaring variables without immediate initialization avoids unnecessary memory allocation until the variable is actually used.

Common Pitfalls to Avoid

Confusing Zero Values With Explicit Initialization While the zero value provides a predictable state, it's important to explicitly initialize variables when the default isn't suitable.

Example:

go

Copy

```
// Potentially confusing

var name string

fmt.Println(name) // Prints "" but might mislead readers into thinking it's uninitialized
```

1. **Overusing Nil** While nil is a valid zero value, overreliance on it can lead to verbose code. Always check whether nil usage is necessary or if a default value would simplify the design.

By embracing the zero value principle, Go developers can write cleaner, safer, and more predictable code. It reduces the cognitive load of managing variable states, making Go code straightforward and reliable.

2.2 Working With Slices, Maps, and Structs Efficiently

Slices, maps, and structs are foundational data structures in Go, each with its own strengths and idiomatic usage patterns. Mastering these data structures is key to writing efficient and idiomatic Go code.

Slices: Go's Flexible Arrays

A slice is a dynamically-sized, flexible view into the elements of an array. Unlike arrays, slices don't have a fixed size, making them ideal for most collection-based operations.

1. **Creating Slices** Slices can be created in several ways:

From an array:

go

Copy

```
arr := [5]int{1, 2, 3, 4, 5}

slice := arr[1:4] // Elements from index 1 to 3

fmt.Println(slice) // Output: [2 3 4]
```

- Using make:

  go

  Copy

  ```
  slice := make([]int, 3) // Creates a slice of length 3

  fmt.Println(slice)    // Output: [0 0 0]
  ```

- **Appending Elements** Use append to dynamically grow a slice:

  go

  Copy

  ```
  slice := []int{1, 2}

  slice = append(slice, 3, 4)

  fmt.Println(slice) // Output: [1 2 3 4]
  ```

2. **Copying Slices** Copying slices is efficient and avoids modifying the original:

go

Copy

```
src := []int{1, 2, 3}

dest := make([]int, len(src))

copy(dest, src)
```

Maps: Key-Value Storage

Maps provide a simple and efficient way to store key-value pairs. They are especially useful for lookups and counting tasks.

Declaring and Initializing Maps

go

Copy

```
ages := map[string]int{

    "Alice": 30,

    "Bob":   25,

}

fmt.Println(ages["Alice"]) // Output: 30
```

1. **Adding and Deleting Keys**

go

Copy

```
ages["Charlie"] = 35     // Add a new key

delete(ages, "Bob")      // Delete a key
```

2. **Checking for Key Existence** Use the "comma ok" idiom to check if a key exists:

go

Copy

```
age, ok := ages["Alice"]

if ok {

    fmt.Printf("Alice is %d years old\n", age)

} else {

    fmt.Println("Alice not found")

}
```

Structs: Custom Data Types

Structs allow developers to define custom data types with named fields. They are essential for modeling real-world entities.

Defining and Using Structs

go

Copy

```
type Person struct {

    Name string

    Age  int

}
```

```go
func main() {

    p := Person{Name: "Alice", Age: 30}

    fmt.Println(p.Name) // Output: Alice

}
```

1. **Embedded Structs** Struct embedding is Go's way of supporting composition:
   go
   Copy

```go
type Employee struct {

Person

ID int

}

func main() {

    e := Employee{Person: Person{Name: "Alice", Age: 30}, ID: 123}

    fmt.Println(e.Name) // Output: Alice

}
```

Performance Considerations

Avoid Over-Allocating Slices Preallocate capacity if the size is known:
go
Copy

```go
slice := make([]int, 0, 100)
```

24

1. **Minimize Map Collisions** Choose appropriate key types to reduce hash collisions and improve performance.
2. **Use Pointers for Large Structs** When passing large structs to functions, use pointers to avoid unnecessary copying.

By understanding and applying idiomatic patterns for slices, maps, and structs, developers can fully utilize Go's capabilities while writing efficient, maintainable code.

You said:

continue with 2.3 Idiomatic Use of Interfaces and Polymorphism 2.4 Writing Clean Loops and Ranges

ChatGPT said:

ChatGPT

2.3 Idiomatic Use of Interfaces and Polymorphism

In Go, interfaces are a cornerstone of the language's design philosophy. Unlike traditional object-oriented programming languages that rely heavily on inheritance, Go uses interfaces to achieve polymorphism and flexibility. The idiomatic use of interfaces allows developers to write modular, maintainable, and testable code.

What Are Interfaces in Go?

An interface in Go is a type that specifies a set of method signatures. Any type that implements these methods automatically satisfies the interface, without the need for explicit declarations. This implicit satisfaction is a hallmark of Go's approach, enabling powerful yet simple design patterns.

Example:

go

Copy

```go
type Speaker interface {
    Speak() string
}
type Dog struct{}
func (d Dog) Speak() string {
    return "Woof!"
}
type Cat struct{}
func (c Cat) Speak() string {
    return "Meow!"
}
func main() {
    var s Speaker
    s = Dog{}
    fmt.Println(s.Speak()) // Output: Woof!
```

```
s = Cat{}

fmt.Println(s.Speak()) // Output: Meow!

}
```

In this example, both Dog and Cat implement the Speaker interface by providing the Speak method. There's no need for explicit declarations, keeping the code clean and focused.

Why Use Interfaces?

1. **Encapsulation of Behavior** Interfaces abstract behavior, allowing you to write code that works with multiple types without knowing their exact implementation.
2. **Decoupling** By programming to an interface instead of a concrete type, you make your code more flexible and easier to change.
3. **Testability** Interfaces make it easier to mock dependencies in tests, as you can provide custom implementations tailored for the test environment.

Example of decoupling:

go

Copy

```
type PaymentProcessor interface {

    ProcessPayment(amount float64) error

}
```

```go
type PayPal struct{}

func (p PayPal) ProcessPayment(amount float64) error {

    fmt.Printf("Processing payment of $%.2f via PayPal\n", amount)

    return nil

}

func Checkout(processor PaymentProcessor, amount float64) {

    err := processor.ProcessPayment(amount)

    if err != nil {

        fmt.Println("Payment failed:", err)

    }

}

func main() {

    p := PayPal{}

    Checkout(p, 50.0)

}
```

Here, the Checkout function operates on the PaymentProcessor interface, allowing you to swap out implementations (e.g., PayPal, Stripe) without changing the function.

Idiomatic Practices for Interfaces

Keep Interfaces Small Interfaces should define only the methods required for a specific use case. The smaller the interface, the easier it is to implement and satisfy.

Example:

go

Copy

```
type Reader interface {

    Read(p []byte) (n int, err error)

}
```

```
type Writer interface {

    Write(p []byte) (n int, err error)

}
```

1. Instead of a monolithic interface like ReaderWriter, Go separates these concerns into Reader and Writer.

Favor Interfaces Over Structs in Function Parameters Accept interfaces where possible, as this allows greater flexibility for function callers.

Example:

go

Copy

```
func PrintMessage(writer Writer, message string) {

    writer.Write([]byte(message))

}
```

29

2. **Use Empty Interface Sparingly** The empty interface (interface{}) can represent any type but should only be used when absolutely necessary, such as in generic libraries or for working with unknown types.

Interface Assertions and Type Switches

Go provides mechanisms to inspect and work with interface types at runtime:

- **Type Assertion**: Retrieve the concrete type of an interface.
- **Type Switch**: Perform actions based on the underlying type.

Example:

go

Copy

```go
func Describe(i interface{}) {

    switch v := i.(type) {

    case string:

        fmt.Printf("String: %s\n", v)

    case int:

        fmt.Printf("Integer: %d\n", v)

    default:

        fmt.Println("Unknown type")

    }
```

}

By combining small, well-defined interfaces with these tools, you can create modular, idiomatic Go programs that are easy to extend and maintain.

2.4 Writing Clean Loops and Ranges

Loops are fundamental in programming, and Go's simple and consistent syntax for loops makes it a standout feature. Unlike many languages that support multiple looping constructs (while, for, do-while), Go has a single for keyword that can handle all looping scenarios. Writing clean loops in Go means using this single construct efficiently and idiomatically.

The Basic For Loop

The traditional for loop in Go resembles that of C-style languages, but it's more streamlined.

Example:

go

Copy

```
for i := 0; i < 10; i++ {

    fmt.Println(i)

}
```

Here's what makes Go's for loop clean:

1. Initialization (i := 0).
2. Condition (i < 10).
3. Post statement (i++).

This format is compact and consistent, ensuring readability and predictability.

Using for as a While Loop

In Go, you can omit parts of the for loop syntax to create a loop that behaves like a while loop:

Example:

go

Copy

```
i := 0

for i < 10 {

    fmt.Println(i)

    i++

}
```

You can even create an infinite loop by omitting the condition entirely:

go

Copy

```go
for {

    fmt.Println("This will run forever!")

}
```

The Range Loop

The range keyword simplifies iterating over collections like slices, arrays, maps, and channels. It provides a clean, idiomatic way to loop through data structures.

Iterating Over a Slice

go
Copy

```go
nums := []int{1, 2, 3, 4, 5}

for i, num := range nums {

    fmt.Printf("Index: %d, Value: %d\n", i, num)

}
```

If you only need the value and not the index, you can use _ to ignore it:
go
Copy

```go
for _, num := range nums {

    fmt.Println(num)

}
```

33

1. **Iterating Over a Map** When iterating over a map, range returns both the key and value:

go
Copy
```go
ages := map[string]int{"Alice": 30, "Bob": 25}

for name, age := range ages {

    fmt.Printf("%s is %d years old\n", name, age)

}
```

2. **Iterating Over Strings** The range loop can also iterate over the runes (Unicode code points) in a string:

go
Copy
```go
s := "hello"

for i, r := range s {

    fmt.Printf("Index: %d, Rune: %c\n", i, r)

}
```

3. **Iterating Over Channels** When reading from a channel, range automatically stops when the channel is closed:

go
Copy
```go
ch := make(chan int)

go func() {

    for i := 1; i <= 3; i++ {

        ch <- i
```

```go
    }

    close(ch)

}()

for num := range ch {

    fmt.Println(num)

}
```

Best Practices for Writing Clean Loops

1. **Avoid Nesting Too Deeply** Complex loops with multiple levels of nesting can become hard to follow. Break them into separate functions or use continue and break to simplify logic.

2. **Use Descriptive Variable Names** Avoid generic names like i or j if they don't convey meaning. Instead, choose names that reflect the purpose of the loop variable.

Keep Loop Logic Simple Complicated conditions or actions within a loop can obscure its purpose. Aim for clarity by minimizing inline calculations or side effects.

Example (non-idiomatic):

go

Copy

```go
for i := 0; i < len(nums) && nums[i] != target; i++ {

    fmt.Println(nums[i])

}
```

Refactored (idiomatic):

go

Copy

```go
for _, num := range nums {

  if num == target {

    break

  }

  fmt.Println(num)

}
```

3. **Prefer range Where Possible** Using range over traditional indexed loops is more idiomatic and reduces the chances of off-by-one errors.

Loops are a fundamental tool in Go, and writing them cleanly and idiomatically ensures your code remains readable and maintainable. Whether you're iterating over slices, maps, or channels, Go provides all the tools needed to do so efficiently and elegantly

2.5 Channels and Goroutines: Communicate, Don't Share Memory

One of Go's defining features is its built-in support for concurrency, centered around **goroutines** and **channels**. These tools allow developers to write highly concurrent and scalable programs without the complexities of traditional threading models. The mantra "communicate, don't share memory" captures the essence of Go's approach to concurrency: instead of using shared memory with locks, goroutines exchange data safely through channels.

Goroutines: Lightweight Threads

Goroutines are Go's lightweight abstraction for threads. They are managed by the Go runtime and are much cheaper than traditional operating system threads, both in terms of memory and creation cost.

To start a goroutine, simply prefix a function call with the go keyword:

Example:

go

Copy

```
package main

import (

    "fmt"

    "time"

)

func sayHello() {

    fmt.Println("Hello!")

}

func main() {

    go sayHello()

    time.Sleep(1 * time.Second) // Wait for the goroutine to finish

}
```

37

In this example, the sayHello function runs concurrently with the main function. The time.Sleep ensures the program doesn't exit before the goroutine completes.

Channels: Safe Communication Between Goroutines

Channels provide a way for goroutines to communicate and synchronize execution. They allow data to be passed safely between goroutines, avoiding the need for locks or other synchronization mechanisms.

Creating a Channel

go

Copy

```
ch := make(chan int) // Create an unbuffered channel of type int
```

1. **Sending and Receiving**

Sending data into a channel:

go

Copy

```
ch <- 42
```

Receiving data from a channel:

go

Copy

```
value := <-ch
```

Example: Basic Channel Communication

go

Copy

```
package main
```

38

```go
import "fmt"

func worker(ch chan int) {

    ch <- 42 // Send a value into the channel

}

func main() {

    ch := make(chan int)

    go worker(ch)

    value := <-ch // Receive the value

    fmt.Println(value) // Output: 42

}
```

Buffered vs. Unbuffered Channels

Channels can be either unbuffered (default) or buffered.

- **Unbuffered Channels:** Block the sender until the receiver is ready, and vice versa.
- **Buffered Channels:** Allow a fixed number of values to be sent without requiring a receiver.

Example of a buffered channel:

go

Copy

```go
ch := make(chan int, 2) // Create a channel with a buffer size of 2

ch <- 1

ch <- 2

fmt.Println(<-ch) // Output: 1

fmt.Println(<-ch) // Output: 2
```

Buffered channels are useful when you want to decouple the sending and receiving operations.

Select: Multiplexing Channels

The select statement allows a goroutine to wait on multiple channel operations. It's a powerful tool for building non-blocking and concurrent systems.

Example:

go

Copy

```go
package main
```

```go
import (

    "fmt"

    "time"

)

func main() {

    ch1 := make(chan string)

    ch2 := make(chan string)

    go func() {

        time.Sleep(1 * time.Second)

        ch1 <- "Message from ch1"

    }()

    go func() {

        time.Sleep(2 * time.Second)

        ch2 <- "Message from ch2"

    }()

    for i := 0; i < 2; i++ {

        select {

        case msg1 := <-ch1:

            fmt.Println(msg1)
```

```
    case msg2 := <-ch2:

        fmt.Println(msg2)

    }

  }

}
```

Output:

csharp

Copy

Message from ch1

Message from ch2

Best Practices for Goroutines and Channels

Close Channels Properly Always close channels when you're done sending data. Receivers can detect a closed channel using a second return value.

Example:

go

Copy

```
close(ch)

value, ok := <-ch

if !ok {

    fmt.Println("Channel closed")
```

```
}
```

1. **Avoid Memory Leaks** Ensure goroutines terminate properly by handling all communication channels and exit conditions.

Use Context for Cancellation Use the context package to manage goroutine lifecycles and cancellations.
Example:
go
Copy

```go
import (

    "context"

    "fmt"

    "time"

)

func main() {

    ctx, cancel := context.WithTimeout(context.Background(), 2*time.Second)

    defer cancel()

    ch := make(chan int)

    go func(ctx context.Context) {

        for {

            select {

            case <-ctx.Done():
```

```
        fmt.Println("Goroutine stopped")

        return

    default:

        fmt.Println("Working...")

        time.Sleep(500 * time.Millisecond)

      }

    }

  }(ctx)

  time.Sleep(3 * time.Second)

}
```

2.6 Composition Over Inheritance: Designing Reusable Code

Go does not have traditional inheritance as seen in object-oriented languages like Java or C++. Instead, Go encourages **composition**, which allows developers to build reusable and modular code by embedding types and combining functionality.

What Is Composition?

Composition is the practice of building complex types by combining simpler ones. Instead of inheriting behavior from a parent class, types can embed other types to gain their functionality.

Example:

go

Copy

```go
type Animal struct {
    Name string
}

func (a Animal) Speak() {
    fmt.Printf("%s makes a noise\n", a.Name)
}

type Dog struct {
    Animal
    Breed string
}

func main() {
    d := Dog{Animal: Animal{Name: "Buddy"}, Breed: "Golden Retriever"}
    d.Speak() // Output: Buddy makes a noise
}
```

In this example, the Dog struct embeds the Animal struct. This allows Dog to inherit the Speak method without requiring an inheritance hierarchy.

Why Composition Over Inheritance?

1. **Flexibility** Composition allows you to mix and match behavior. A type can embed multiple other types, gaining their functionality without being locked into a rigid hierarchy.
2. **Simplicity** Inheritance often leads to deep and complex hierarchies, which can be hard to manage. Composition keeps the design flat and easier to understand.
3. **Decoupling** By favoring composition, you can create smaller, reusable components that don't rely on a tightly coupled relationship.

Embedding in Practice

Method Promotion Embedded types promote their methods to the embedding type, making them accessible without additional code.

Example:

go

Copy

```go
type Logger struct{}

func (l Logger) Log(message string) {

    fmt.Println("LOG:", message)

}

type Service struct {

    Logger
```

```go
}

func main() {

    s := Service{}

    s.Log("Starting service...") // Output: LOG: Starting service...

}
```

1. **Overriding Behavior** The embedding type can define methods with the same name as the embedded type, effectively overriding the behavior.
   Example:
   go
   Copy

```go
type Animal struct{}

func (a Animal) Speak() {

    fmt.Println("Animal speaks")

}

type Dog struct {

    Animal

}

func (d Dog) Speak() {

    fmt.Println("Dog barks")

}
```

```go
func main() {

    d := Dog{}

    d.Speak() // Output: Dog barks

}
```

2. Composition vs. Interfaces

Composition and interfaces often work hand-in-hand in Go. While composition provides concrete functionality, interfaces define the expected behavior.

Example:

go

Copy

```go
type Mover interface {

    Move()

}

type Engine struct{}

func (e Engine) Move() {

    fmt.Println("Engine is moving")

}


type Car struct {
```

```
    Engine

}

func main() {

    var m Mover = Car{}

    m.Move() // Output: Engine is moving

}
```

Here, the Car type satisfies the Mover interface through its embedded Engine.

Best Practices for Composition

1. **Favor Small, Focused Types** Create small types that encapsulate specific functionality and embed them as needed.
2. **Use Embedding Judiciously** Avoid over-embedding types to prevent confusing behavior or accidental method overrides.
3. **Combine Composition and Interfaces** Use interfaces to define expected behavior and composition to share concrete implementations.

By emphasizing composition over inheritance and leveraging idiomatic practices like goroutines and channels, Go provides a clean, scalable way to design reusable and concurrent systems. These approaches ensure maintainability, simplicity, and performance in modern applications.

Chapter 3: Error Handling and Debugging

3.1 Go's Philosophy of Error Handling: if err != nil

Error handling is a central aspect of programming, and Go takes a distinctive approach by treating errors as values rather than exceptions. This approach encourages developers to handle errors explicitly and immediately, resulting in clear and predictable code.

The Basics of Error Handling in Go

In Go, errors are represented by the built-in error type, which is simply an interface:

go

Copy

```
type error interface {

    Error() string

}
```

This means that any type implementing the Error() method satisfies the error interface, allowing developers to create custom error types as needed.

The most common idiom in Go for error handling is:

go

Copy

```
if err != nil {

    return err
```

}

Why Go Favors Explicit Error Handling

1. **Clarity and Simplicity** Errors in Go are not hidden behind complex mechanisms like exceptions. Instead, they are handled explicitly at the point where they occur, making the flow of error handling straightforward and predictable.
2. **Avoids Silent Failures** Explicit error checking ensures that errors are not accidentally ignored. This leads to more robust and reliable code.
3. **Encourages Granular Handling** By treating errors as first-class values, Go enables developers to differentiate between types of errors and respond to them appropriately.

Anatomy of Error Handling in Go

Checking Errors A typical Go function that performs an operation and returns an error looks like this:

go

Copy

```go
func divide(a, b int) (int, error) {

    if b == 0 {

        return 0, fmt.Errorf("cannot divide by zero")

    }

    return a / b, nil

}
```

```
func main() {

    result, err := divide(10, 0)

    if err != nil {

        fmt.Println("Error:", err)

        return

    }

    fmt.Println("Result:", result)

}
```

Output:

vbnet

Copy

Error: cannot divide by zero

1. **Returning Errors** When a function encounters an error, it should return it to the caller for further handling. This allows errors to propagate up the call stack in a controlled manner.

Creating Custom Error Types

Sometimes, a simple error message isn't enough. You may need to include additional context or differentiate between error types. To achieve this, you can define custom error types:

Example:

go

Copy

```go
type DivideError struct {

    Dividend int

    Divisor  int

}

func (e DivideError) Error() string {

    return fmt.Sprintf("cannot divide %d by %d", e.Dividend, e.Divisor)

}


func divide(a, b int) (int, error) {

    if b == 0 {

        return 0, DivideError{Dividend: a, Divisor: b}

    }

    return a / b, nil

}


func main() {
```

```go
    _, err := divide(10, 0)

    if err != nil {

        fmt.Println("Error:", err)

    }

}
```

Output:

vbnet

Copy

Error: cannot divide 10 by 0

Common Patterns for Error Handling

Wrapping Errors Add context to an existing error using fmt.Errorf with the %w verb:

go

Copy

```go
if err != nil {

    return fmt.Errorf("operation failed: %w", err)

}
```

1. **Unwrapping Errors** Use the errors package to inspect and unwrap errors:

go

Copy

```go
import "errors"



if errors.Is(err, targetError) {

    fmt.Println("Target error occurred")

}



if unwrappedErr := errors.Unwrap(err); unwrappedErr != nil {

    fmt.Println("Unwrapped error:", unwrappedErr)

}
```

2. **Sentinel Errors** Use predefined var declarations for commonly expected errors:

go

Copy

```go
var ErrNotFound = errors.New("not found")



func lookup(key string) error {

    return ErrNotFound

}
```

```go
func main() {

    err := lookup("key")

    if errors.Is(err, ErrNotFound) {

        fmt.Println("Key not found")

    }

}
```

When to Ignore Errors

While Go encourages handling errors explicitly, there are rare cases where it's acceptable to ignore errors. Use _ to explicitly discard errors:

go

Copy

```go
result, _ := strconv.Atoi("123")
```

Only do this when the context guarantees the operation won't fail.

Best Practices

1. **Handle Errors Close to Their Source** Check errors immediately after they occur to make debugging easier.
2. **Provide Context** Add meaningful messages to errors to make them informative for developers.

3. **Don't Overuse** panic Reserve panic for truly exceptional situations where the program cannot continue safely.

3.2 The Proper Use of defer, recover, and panic

Go's error handling philosophy is built around explicit checks, but there are situations where you may need to recover from an unexpected error or clean up resources. This is where defer, recover, and panic come into play.

---

defer: Ensuring Cleanup

The defer keyword schedules a function to run after the current function completes. It is often used for cleanup tasks like closing files or releasing resources.

Example:

go

Copy

```go
func readFile(filename string) {
    file, err := os.Open(filename)
    if err != nil {
        fmt.Println("Error opening file:", err)
        return
    }
}
```

```go
defer file.Close() // Ensures the file is closed

    // Process the file

    fmt.Println("Reading file:", filename)

}
```

Key Points:

1. Deferred functions execute in **LIFO order** (last-in, first-out).
2. Use defer to simplify cleanup logic and avoid resource leaks.

Example with multiple defers:

go

Copy

```go
func main() {

    defer fmt.Println("First deferred")

    defer fmt.Println("Second deferred")

    fmt.Println("Main function")

}
```

Output:

sql

Main function

Second deferred

First deferred

---

panic: Signaling Exceptional Conditions

The panic function stops the normal execution of a program and begins unwinding the stack, calling all deferred functions along the way. It is used to signal a critical, unrecoverable error.

Example:

go

```go
func divide(a, b int) int {
   if b == 0 {
      panic("cannot divide by zero")
   }
   return a / b
}
```

```
func main() {

    fmt.Println(divide(10, 0)) // Program will panic

}
```

Use panic sparingly and only for truly exceptional situations, such as:

- Program invariants being violated.
- Critical errors that cannot be recovered from.

---

recover: Catching a Panic

The recover function allows you to regain control after a panic, but it must be called within a deferred function. This makes it possible to gracefully handle panics and prevent the program from crashing.

Example:

go

Copy

```
func safeDivide(a, b int) {

    defer func() {

        if r := recover(); r != nil {

            fmt.Println("Recovered from panic:", r)

        }

    }()
```

```go
    fmt.Println(a / b)

}


func main() {

    safeDivide(10, 0) // Recovered from panic: cannot divide by zero

    fmt.Println("Program continues")

}
```

Best Practices for defer, recover, and panic

1. **Use defer for Cleanup**
   - Always defer resource cleanup (e.g., closing files, releasing locks) to prevent leaks.
2. **Minimize panic Usage**
   - Avoid panicking for normal error conditions; use error values instead.
3. **Handle Panics Gracefully**
   - Use recover to catch panics and log or handle them appropriately.

Common Anti-Patterns to Avoid

Overusing panic Using panic for non-critical errors can make the program harder to debug and maintain.

go

Copy

```
// Non-idiomatic

if err != nil {

    panic(err)

}
```

Instead, return the error to the caller.

go

Copy

```
if err != nil {

    return err

}
```

1. **Ignoring defer in Cleanup** Forgetting to use defer can lead to resource leaks or inconsistent state.
2. **Unnecessary recover** Use recover only when you truly need to regain control after a panic. Don't rely on it as a substitute for proper error handling.

By combining explicit error handling (if err != nil) with the judicious use of defer, panic, and recover, you can write robust, maintainable Go programs. This balanced approach ensures that your code is both predictable and resilient in the face of unexpected conditions.

3.3 Debugging Tools and Best Practices

Debugging is an essential part of software development, and Go provides a variety of tools and techniques to help developers identify and resolve issues in their code. By understanding and effectively using these tools, you can streamline the debugging process and maintain code quality.

Go's Built-In Debugging Tools

fmt.Printf for Debugging While primitive, using fmt.Printf statements can help quickly trace the flow of execution and identify problematic values.

Example:

go

Copy

```go
func divide(a, b int) int {

    fmt.Printf("divide called with a=%d, b=%d\n", a, b)

    return a / b

}

func main() {

    fmt.Println(divide(10, 0)) // Debug message printed before the error

}
```

1. Use this approach for simple, temporary debugging needs. Avoid leaving these statements in production code.

The log Package The log package provides a more robust way to log messages with timestamps.

Example:

go

```
import "log"

func main() {

    log.Println("This is a log message")

    log.Fatalf("Critical error: %s", "something went wrong")

}
```

2. Key features:
   - log.Println: Logs a message with a timestamp.
   - log.Fatalf: Logs a message and exits the program.
   - log.SetOutput: Directs logs to a file or another output stream.

The pprof Tool The pprof package helps identify performance bottlenecks, such as excessive memory usage or CPU cycles.

Example of CPU profiling:

go

```
import (

    "os"

    "runtime/pprof"

)
```

```
func main() {

    f, _ := os.Create("cpu.prof")

    pprof.StartCPUProfile(f)

    defer pprof.StopCPUProfile()


    // Code to profile

}
```

Analyze the generated profile using the pprof command-line tool:

sh

Copy

```
go tool pprof cpu.prof
```

The delve Debugger delve is a powerful debugger specifically designed for Go. It supports breakpoints, variable inspection, and step-through debugging.

To install delve:

sh

Copy

```
go install github.com/go-delve/delve/cmd/dlv@latest
```

Example usage:

sh

Copy

```
dlv debug main.go
```

4. Key commands in delve:
    o break [line/function]: **Set a breakpoint.**

- ○ continue: Resume program execution.
- ○ next: Move to the next statement.
- ○ print [variable]: Inspect a variable's value.

Debugging Best Practices

1. **Write Clear and Readable Code** Well-written code is easier to debug. Use meaningful variable names, avoid overly complex logic, and adhere to Go's idiomatic practices.
2. **Test Continuously** Writing unit tests and integration tests can help catch errors early, reducing the need for extensive debugging later.
3. **Use Context-Rich Logging** Include relevant details in your logs, such as function names, parameters, and timestamps. Structured logging (e.g., using logrus or zap) can further improve log clarity.

Leverage Go's Race Detector The race detector identifies data race conditions in concurrent code.

Example:

sh

Copy

```
go run -race main.go
```

4. **Reproduce Issues** Reproduce the bug in a controlled environment before attempting to fix it. This ensures you're addressing the root cause.
5. **Isolate Problematic Code** Use breakpoints or logging to narrow down the part of the code responsible for the issue. Avoid making assumptions about where the problem lies.
6. **Use Tools Like Static Analyzers** Tools like golangci-lint and go vet catch common mistakes and potential issues during development.

3.4 Common Error Handling Anti-Patterns

Even though Go's error handling philosophy is straightforward, developers often fall into certain traps when implementing error handling. Avoiding these anti-patterns ensures your code remains clean, maintainable, and aligned with Go's idioms.

---

1. Ignoring Errors

One of the most common mistakes is ignoring returned errors. This leaves potential issues unaddressed and can lead to unpredictable behavior.

Example:

go

Copy

```go
file, _ := os.Open("config.json") // Error ignored
defer file.Close()
```

Fix: Always check and handle errors, even if it's just logging them:

go

Copy

```go
file, err := os.Open("config.json")
if err != nil {
```

```
    log.Fatalf("Failed to open file: %v", err)

}

defer file.Close()
```

---

2. Overusing panic

panic is meant for critical errors, such as violations of program invariants, and should not be used for general error handling.

Example:

go

Copy

```
if err != nil {

    panic("Something went wrong")

}
```

Fix: Return errors to the caller instead of panicking:

go

Copy

```
if err != nil {
```

```go
        return fmt.Errorf("operation failed: %w", err)

}
```

---

3. Nesting Too Many if err != nil Blocks

Excessive error-checking blocks can make the code difficult to read and maintain.

Example:

go

Copy

```go
func process() error {

    file, err := os.Open("config.json")

    if err != nil {

        return err

    }

    defer file.Close()


    data, err := ioutil.ReadAll(file)

    if err != nil {

        return err
```

69

```go
    }

    err = processData(data)

    if err != nil {

        return err

    }


    return nil

}
```

Fix: Use helper functions or early returns to reduce nesting:

go

Copy

```go
func process() error {

    file, err := os.Open("config.json")

    if err != nil {

        return fmt.Errorf("failed to open file: %w", err)

    }

    defer file.Close()
```

```go
data, err := ioutil.ReadAll(file)

if err != nil {

    return fmt.Errorf("failed to read file: %w", err)

}


if err := processData(data); err != nil {

    return fmt.Errorf("failed to process data: %w", err)

}


return nil

}
```

---

4. Returning Uninformative Errors

Generic error messages make debugging difficult, especially in large codebases.

Example:

go

Copy

```
return errors.New("something went wrong")
```

Fix: Add context to errors using fmt.Errorf or custom error types:

go

Copy

```
return fmt.Errorf("failed to process file %s: %w", filename, err)
```

---

5. Not Wrapping Errors

Failing to wrap errors makes it hard to trace the origin of an error when it propagates through multiple function calls.

Example:

go

Copy

```
return err
```

Fix: Always wrap errors with additional context:

go

Copy

72

```go
return fmt.Errorf("database query failed: %w", err)
```

---

6. Using defer Incorrectly

Deferred calls should be used for cleanup tasks but can lead to unexpected behavior if misused.

Example:

go

Copy

```go
for i := 0; i < 5; i++ {

    defer fmt.Println(i) // Prints in reverse order

}
```

Fix: Understand the order of deferred calls and avoid using defer in loops unless necessary.

---

7. Overcomplicating Error Handling

Introducing unnecessary abstractions for errors can make the code harder to read and maintain.

73

Example:

go

Copy

```go
type CustomError struct {

    Message string

}


func (e CustomError) Error() string {

    return e.Message

}
```

Fix: Use Go's standard error interface unless there's a strong reason to create custom error types.

Best Practices for Error Handling

1. **Be Consistent** Follow a consistent error-handling pattern throughout your codebase.
2. **Prioritize Readability** Keep error-handling logic clear and concise.
3. **Use Go's Tools** Leverage go vet, linters, and static analysis tools to catch common error-handling mistakes.
4. **Fail Fast** Return errors as soon as they are detected, and avoid continuing operations in an invalid state.

74

By using Go's debugging tools and avoiding common error-handling anti-patterns, you can write robust, maintainable, and error-resistant code. These practices will help you effectively address issues during development and production.

Chapter 4: Concurrency Made Simple

4.1 Introduction to Goroutines and How They Work

Concurrency is one of Go's standout features, designed to handle multiple tasks efficiently and with minimal complexity. At the heart of Go's concurrency model are **goroutines**—lightweight, managed threads that allow programs to run tasks concurrently without the overhead of traditional operating system threads.

What Are Goroutines?

A **goroutine** is a function that runs concurrently with other functions. It's like a thread, but it's much lighter and managed entirely by the Go runtime. Goroutines use a fraction of the memory required for OS threads, allowing Go to scale to thousands or even millions of goroutines within a single program.

To start a goroutine, use the go keyword before a function call.

Example:

go

Copy

```
package main

import (

    "fmt"
```

```go
    "time"
)


func sayHello() {

    fmt.Println("Hello!")

}


func main() {

    go sayHello() // Start a new goroutine

    time.Sleep(1 * time.Second) // Allow time for the goroutine to finish

    fmt.Println("Main function")

}
```

Output:

bash

Copy

```
Hello!

Main function
```

In this example, sayHello runs concurrently with the main function. The time.Sleep ensures the program doesn't terminate before the goroutine completes.

Key Features of Goroutines

1. **Lightweight** Unlike OS threads, goroutines start with a small amount of stack memory (typically 2 KB) and grow as needed. This efficiency allows Go programs to handle massive concurrency.
2. **Non-Blocking** Goroutines execute independently and don't block other goroutines or the main function.
3. **Managed by the Runtime** The Go runtime handles scheduling and managing goroutines, so developers don't need to worry about thread pools or manual context switching.

Launching Goroutines

Using Anonymous Functions Goroutines can be launched with anonymous functions for inline tasks.

go
Copy

```go
go func(name string) {

    fmt.Printf("Hello, %s!\n", name)

}("Gopher")
```

1. **Concurrent Iterations** Be cautious when launching goroutines inside loops. Capture loop variables correctly to avoid unexpected behavior.
   go

```
Copy
for i := 0; i < 5; i++ {

go func(n int) {

    fmt.Println(n)

}(i) // Pass loop variable as an argument

}
```

Challenges With Goroutines

Uncoordinated Termination Goroutines run independently, so if the main function exits, all running goroutines are terminated.

go
Copy
```
go func() {

    fmt.Println("This may never print")

}()
```

1. **Solution:** Use synchronization tools like WaitGroup to ensure goroutines complete before the program exits.
2. **Resource Contention** Goroutines sharing resources can lead to race conditions. Use synchronization mechanisms like mutexes or channels to manage access safely.
3. **Leakage** Goroutines may leak if they block indefinitely (e.g., waiting on a channel that never receives data). Always design goroutines with clear exit conditions.

Best Practices for Using Goroutines

1. Use goroutines for tasks that are independent and can run concurrently.
2. Avoid starting too many goroutines without understanding their resource usage.
3. Combine goroutines with synchronization tools (e.g., channels, sync package) for coordination.

4.2 The sync Package: Mutexes, WaitGroups, and More

While goroutines provide the building blocks for concurrency, Go's sync **package** offers tools for managing synchronization and shared resources effectively. Key tools in this package include **mutexes**, **WaitGroups**, and other primitives to coordinate goroutines and prevent race conditions.

---

1. Mutex: Preventing Race Conditions

A **mutex** (short for mutual exclusion) ensures that only one goroutine can access a shared resource at a time. This prevents race conditions, where multiple goroutines modify the same variable simultaneously.

Example:

go

Copy

```
package main


import (
```

```go
    "fmt"

    "sync"

)


func main() {

    var mu sync.Mutex

    counter := 0


    for i := 0; i < 5; i++ {

        go func() {

            mu.Lock() // Lock the critical section

            counter++

            mu.Unlock() // Unlock after modifying

        }()

    }


    fmt.Println("Final counter:", counter) // This might still be unpredictable!

}
```

Key Points:

- Always call mu.Unlock() after mu.Lock(), even in cases of errors or panics (use defer to ensure this).
- Use mutexes for small, critical sections to minimize contention and improve performance.

---

2. WaitGroup: Synchronizing Goroutines

A **WaitGroup** waits for a collection of goroutines to complete before proceeding. It is useful when you need to ensure that all goroutines finish before the main function exits.

Example:

go

Copy

```
package main

import (

    "fmt"

    "sync"

)


func worker(id int, wg *sync.WaitGroup) {

    defer wg.Done() // Notify WaitGroup when done
```

```go
    fmt.Printf("Worker %d starting\n", id)

    // Simulate work

    fmt.Printf("Worker %d done\n", id)

}


func main() {

    var wg sync.WaitGroup


    for i := 1; i <= 3; i++ {

        wg.Add(1) // Increment WaitGroup counter

        go worker(i, &wg)

    }


    wg.Wait() // Block until all workers are done

    fmt.Println("All workers completed")

}
```

Output:

bash

83

Copy

Worker 1 starting

Worker 2 starting

Worker 3 starting

Worker 1 done

Worker 2 done

Worker 3 done

All workers completed   .

---

3. Once: Ensuring One-Time Initialization

The sync.Once type guarantees that a piece of code runs only once, no matter how many goroutines invoke it.

Example:

go

Copy

```
package main


import (

    "fmt"
```

```go
    "sync"
)

func main() {
    var once sync.Once
    initFunc := func() {
        fmt.Println("Initialized")
    }

    for i := 0; i < 3; i++ {
        go once.Do(initFunc)
    }
}
```

Output:

Copy

Initialized

---

4. RWMutex: Optimizing Read-Write Access

The sync.RWMutex is a variation of the mutex that allows multiple readers or one writer at a time. It is ideal for scenarios where read-heavy workloads dominate.

Example:

go

Copy

```go
package main

import (
    "fmt"
    "sync"
)

func main() {
    var rw sync.RWMutex
    data := 0

    // Reader goroutine
    go func() {
```

```go
    rw.RLock()

    fmt.Println("Reading data:", data)

    rw.RUnlock()

}()

// Writer goroutine

go func() {

    rw.Lock()

    data = 42

    fmt.Println("Writing data:", data)

    rw.Unlock()

}()

}
```

---

5. Cond: Broadcast Notifications

A sync.Cond allows goroutines to signal and wait for events. It is useful when coordinating complex goroutine workflows.

Example:

go

Copy

```go
package main

import (

    "fmt"

    "sync"

)


func main() {

    cond := sync.NewCond(&sync.Mutex{})

    ready := false


    go func() {

        cond.L.Lock()

        for !ready {

            cond.Wait() // Wait for a signal

        }

        fmt.Println("Signal received!")

        cond.L.Unlock()

    }()
```

```
cond.L.Lock()

ready = true

cond.Signal() // Notify one waiting goroutine

cond.L.Unlock()

}
```

Best Practices for Using the sync Package

1. **Minimize Lock Duration** Keep critical sections small to reduce contention.
2. **Avoid Deadlocks** Deadlocks occur when multiple goroutines block each other indefinitely. Design locking strategies carefully to prevent circular dependencies.
3. **Prefer Higher-Level Abstractions** Use channels or other synchronization mechanisms when possible, as they are more idiomatic in Go.
4. **Use sync.Once for Global Initialization** For initializing shared resources, sync.Once is safer and more concise than manual checks.

With goroutines and the sync package, Go provides powerful tools to build concurrent systems. By understanding how to use these tools effectively, you can write robust, efficient, and maintainable code that takes full advantage of Go's concurrency capabilities.

4.3 Patterns for Effective Concurrency

Concurrency in Go becomes significantly more powerful and maintainable when developers apply well-established patterns. By structuring concurrent code with patterns like **worker pools**, **fan-out/fan-in**, and **pipelines**, you can design scalable, efficient, and idiomatic solutions for real-world problems.

Worker Pools

A worker pool is a concurrency pattern that involves a fixed number of worker goroutines processing tasks from a shared queue. This is particularly useful for controlling the number of concurrent operations and efficiently utilizing resources.

How It Works:

- A channel serves as the task queue.
- Worker goroutines read tasks from the channel and process them.
- The main goroutine adds tasks to the channel and waits for the workers to complete.

Example:

go

Copy

```go
package main

import (

    "fmt"

    "sync"

    "time"
```

```go
)

func worker(id int, tasks <-chan int, wg *sync.WaitGroup) {
    defer wg.Done()
    for task := range tasks {
        fmt.Printf("Worker %d processing task %d\n", id, task)
        time.Sleep(time.Second) // Simulate work
    }
}

func main() {
    const numWorkers = 3
    tasks := make(chan int, 10)
    var wg sync.WaitGroup

    // Start worker goroutines
    for i := 1; i <= numWorkers; i++ {
        wg.Add(1)
        go worker(i, tasks, &wg)
```

```
}

// Send tasks to the workers

for i := 1; i <= 10; i++ {

    tasks <- i

}

close(tasks) // Signal that no more tasks will be sent

wg.Wait() // Wait for all workers to finish

fmt.Println("All tasks completed")

}
```

Benefits of Worker Pools:

1. Controls the number of concurrent goroutines.
2. Prevents resource exhaustion by limiting parallelism.
3. Simplifies task distribution and synchronization.

Fan-Out/Fan-In

Fan-out and fan-in are patterns for distributing and collecting data across multiple goroutines.

1. **Fan-Out**: A single producer sends tasks to multiple worker goroutines.
2. **Fan-In**: Multiple workers send their results to a single channel for aggregation.

Example:

go

Copy

```go
package main

import (
    "fmt"
    "sync"
)

func worker(id int, tasks <-chan int, results chan<- int) {
    for task := range tasks {
        fmt.Printf("Worker %d processing task %d\n", id, task)
        results <- task * 2 // Simulate processing
    }
}

func main() {
    tasks := make(chan int, 10)
```

```go
    results := make(chan int, 10)

    // Start worker goroutines
    for i := 1; i <= 3; i++ {

        go worker(i, tasks, results)

    }

    // Send tasks
    for i := 1; i <= 5; i++ {

        tasks <- i

    }
    close(tasks)

    // Collect results
    for i := 1; i <= 5; i++ {

        fmt.Println("Result:", <-results)

    }
}
```

Advantages:

- Efficiently distributes workload across multiple goroutines.
- Aggregates results for further processing.

Pipelines

Pipelines process data through a series of stages, with each stage running in its own goroutine. Data flows through channels, making the pipeline concurrent and modular.

Example:

go

Copy

```go
package main

import "fmt"

func generateNumbers(nums chan<- int) {
    for i := 1; i <= 5; i++ {
        nums <- i
    }
    close(nums)
}
```

```go
func squareNumbers(nums <-chan int, squares chan<- int) {

    for num := range nums {

        squares <- num * num

    }

    close(squares)

}


func main() {

    nums := make(chan int)

    squares := make(chan int)


    go generateNumbers(nums)

    go squareNumbers(nums, squares)


    for square := range squares {

        fmt.Println("Square:", square)

    }

}
```

Advantages:

- Decouples processing stages, making the code more modular.
- Each stage can run concurrently, improving throughput.

4.4 Avoiding Deadlocks and Race Conditions

Concurrency introduces challenges like deadlocks and race conditions, which can cause unpredictable behavior and make debugging difficult. Understanding how to avoid these issues is critical for writing safe concurrent code.

Deadlocks

A **deadlock** occurs when two or more goroutines are waiting on each other to release resources, preventing further progress.

Example of Deadlock:

go

Copy

```
var mu1, mu2 sync.Mutex


func main() {

    go func() {
```

```
    mu1.Lock()

    defer mu1.Unlock()

    mu2.Lock()

    defer mu2.Unlock()

}()

mu2.Lock()

defer mu2.Unlock()

mu1.Lock()

defer mu1.Unlock()

}
```

How to Avoid Deadlocks:

1. Always acquire locks in a consistent order.
2. Minimize the scope of locks to reduce contention.
3. Use higher-level abstractions like channels instead of mutexes.

Race Conditions

A **race condition** occurs when two or more goroutines access a shared resource simultaneously, and at least one of them modifies it.

Example of Race Condition:

```go
package main

import (
    "fmt"
    "sync"
)

func main() {
    var counter int
    var wg sync.WaitGroup
    for i := 0; i < 10; i++ {
        wg.Add(1)
        go func() {
            counter++ // Potential race condition
            wg.Done()
        }()
    }
    wg.Wait()
    fmt.Println("Counter:", counter) // Result is unpredictable
```

99

}

How to Avoid Race Conditions:

Use mutexes to protect shared resources:

go

Copy

```
var mu sync.Mutex

mu.Lock()

counter++

mu.Unlock()
```

1. Use channels for synchronization.

Use the -race flag to detect race conditions:

sh

Copy

```
go run -race main.go
```

4.5 Using the context Package for Managing Goroutines

The context **package** is a powerful tool for managing goroutines, especially when you need to propagate deadlines, cancellations, or other signals across goroutines.

Why Use context?

- Prevent goroutines from running indefinitely.
- Propagate cancellation signals to child goroutines.
- Manage deadlines for time-sensitive tasks.

Creating a Context

Background Context: The root context, often used as a base.

go

Copy

```
ctx := context.Background()
```

1. **WithCancel**: Creates a cancellable context.

   go

   Copy

   ```
   ctx, cancel := context.WithCancel(context.Background())
   ```

   ```
   defer cancel()
   ```

2. **WithTimeout**: Adds a timeout to a context.

   go

   Copy

   ```
   ctx, cancel := context.WithTimeout(context.Background(), 2*time.Second)
   ```

   ```
   defer cancel()
   ```

3. **WithValue**: Attaches key-value pairs to a context.

   go

   Copy

   ```
   ctx := context.WithValue(context.Background(), "key", "value")
   ```

Example: Using context for Cancellation

go

Copy

```go
package main

import (

    "context"

    "fmt"

    "time"

)

func worker(ctx context.Context) {

    for {

        select {

        case <-ctx.Done():

            fmt.Println("Worker stopped")

            return

        default:

            fmt.Println("Worker running")

            time.Sleep(500 * time.Millisecond)

        }

    }

}
```

```go
func main() {

    ctx, cancel := context.WithTimeout(context.Background(), 2*time.Second)

    defer cancel()

    go worker(ctx)

    time.Sleep(3 * time.Second)

    fmt.Println("Main function completed")

}
```

Output:

lua

Copy

```
Worker running

Worker running

Worker stopped

Main function completed
```

Best Practices for Using context

1. **Always Cancel Contexts**: Use defer cancel() to release resources.
2. **Pass Context Explicitly**: Always pass context as the first parameter in functions.

3. **Avoid Overusing** WithValue: Use WithValue sparingly and for request-scoped data only.

By applying concurrency patterns, avoiding pitfalls like deadlocks and race conditions, and leveraging the context package, you can write efficient and reliable concurrent Go programs. These tools and techniques ensure that your applications remain scalable and maintainable

Chapter 5: Code Organization and Project Structure

Effective code organization and project structure are essential for creating maintainable, scalable, and collaborative Go applications. Go's module system and package structure provide a clear and consistent way to manage codebases, especially as they grow in size and complexity.

5.1 Organizing Projects With Go Modules and Packages

Go's modular approach and package system are designed to simplify project organization while promoting code reuse and clarity.

Go Modules: A Foundation for Modern Project Management

Introduced in Go 1.11 and made the default in Go 1.13, Go modules provide a robust system for managing dependencies and versioning. A module is a collection of related Go packages defined by a go.mod file at its root.

Steps to Initialize a Module:

Navigate to your project directory:
sh
Copy
```
cd ~/myproject
```

1. Initialize a new module:
   sh
   Copy
   ```
   go mod init github.com/username/myproject
   ```

2. This creates a go.mod file with your module path.
3. Build or run your code. Dependencies will be automatically added to the go.mod file.

Example Project Structure

A well-organized Go project typically adheres to this structure:

go

Copy

myproject/

├── go.mod

├── go.sum

├── cmd/

│   └── myapp/

│   └── main.go

├── pkg/

│   ├── utils/

│   │   └── math.go

│   └── models/

│   └── user.go

├── internal/

```
|   |—— auth/
|   |   └── jwt.go
|   └── db/
|       └── database.go
|—— configs/
|   └── config.yaml
|—— docs/
|   └── README.md
└── tests/
    └── integration_test.go
```

Key Directories:

- cmd/: Contains entry points for your application (e.g., main.go for executables).
- pkg/: Houses reusable packages that can be imported by other projects.
- internal/: Stores private code that should only be accessed within the current module.
- configs/: Configuration files for your application.
- tests/: Test-specific code and test cases.
- docs/: Documentation for the project.

Go Packages: Modular and Reusable Code

Packages are the building blocks of Go projects. Each directory with a .go file is considered a package.

Creating a Package Create a new directory and add .go files with the same package declaration:

go
Copy

```
// utils/math.go

package utils

func Add(a, b int) int {

    return a + b

}
```

1. **Using a Package** Import the package in your code:

    go
    Copy

    ```
    package main

    import (

        "fmt"

        "github.com/username/myproject/pkg/utils"

    )

    func main() {

        fmt.Println(utils.Add(2, 3)) // Output: 5

    }
    ```

Best Practices for Organizing Projects

1. **Keep It Flat and Modular** Avoid deeply nested directories. Group related code into meaningful packages.
2. **Use Descriptive Package Names** Package names should be short and reflect their purpose (e.g., auth, db).
3. **Separate Internal and Public Code** Use the internal/ directory for private code and pkg/ for reusable public packages.
4. **Document Your Code** Add comments to explain the purpose and usage of your packages and functions.
5. **Structure for Growth** Plan your project structure with scalability in mind, especially for larger applications.

5.2 Dependency Management: go mod and Vendoring

Managing dependencies efficiently is critical for ensuring reproducible builds and avoiding compatibility issues. Go's module system (go mod) and support for vendoring make dependency management straightforward.

---

go mod: Managing Dependencies

The go mod tool handles dependency tracking and versioning in Go projects. It works in tandem with the go.mod and go.sum files.

1. **go.mod File**
   - Created with go mod init, it specifies the module path and dependencies.

Example:

bash

Copy

```
module github.com/username/myproject

go 1.20

require (

  github.com/gin-gonic/gin v1.7.4

  golang.org/x/crypto v0.0.0-20230503212524-abc123

)
```

2. **go.sum File**
   - Automatically generated and updated by Go, it records the checksums of module versions for verification.

Adding Dependencies Dependencies are automatically added to go.mod when you build or run your project:
sh
Copy

```
go get github.com/gin-gonic/gin
```

3. **Upgrading or Downgrading Dependencies** Use go get with a specific version to change dependencies:
   sh
   Copy

   ```
   go get github.com/gin-gonic/gin@v1.8.0
   ```

4. **Tidying Up Dependencies** Remove unused dependencies and ensure go.mod is clean:
   sh
   Copy

   ```
   go mod tidy
   ```

5. **Downloading Dependencies** Fetch all dependencies specified in go.mod:

sh

Copy

```
go mod download
```

Vendoring Dependencies

Vendoring allows you to store a copy of your dependencies locally, ensuring your project builds even if external repositories become unavailable.

Enable Vendoring Initialize a vendor/ directory:

sh

Copy

```
go mod vendor
```

1. **Using the Vendor Directory** Build or run your project with the -mod=vendor flag to prioritize local copies:

sh

Copy

```
go build -mod=vendor
```

2. **When to Use Vendoring**
   - Projects with strict dependency control requirements.
   - Applications where internet access is restricted (e.g., offline builds).

Best Practices for Dependency Management

1. **Pin Versions** Always specify exact versions or tags in go.mod to avoid unexpected changes.

2. **Audit Dependencies** Regularly review and update dependencies to address security vulnerabilities and bugs.
3. **Avoid Over-Reliance on Dependencies** Use dependencies sparingly. Prefer Go's standard library where possible.
4. **Use go mod tidy Regularly** Clean up unused dependencies to keep go.mod and go.sum files accurate.
5. **Document External Dependencies** List major dependencies and their purpose in the project documentation for clarity.

Go's module system and package organization make it easy to manage dependencies and structure projects in a clean, scalable way. By following best practices, you can maintain a robust codebase that is easy to collaborate on, scale, and maintain over time.

5.3 Writing Readable and Maintainable Code

Readable and maintainable code is the backbone of successful software projects. It allows teams to collaborate effectively, simplifies debugging, and ensures the longevity of a project. Go's philosophy of simplicity and clarity aligns perfectly with best practices for writing such code.

Key Principles for Readable and Maintainable Code

Keep It Simple Go emphasizes simplicity. Avoid overengineering or adding unnecessary abstractions. The goal is to write code that's easy to understand at a glance. Example (Non-idiomatic):

go

Copy

```
func calcArea(width int, height int) int {
```

```go
return func() int {

    return width * height

}()

}
```

Refactored (Idiomatic):
go
Copy
```go
func calcArea(width, height int) int {

    return width * height

}
```

1. **Use Descriptive Names** Variable, function, and type names should clearly reflect their purpose.

   - **Bad:** func a(b int) int
   - **Good:** func calculateTotal(price int) int

2. **Tip:** Stick to Go's naming conventions:
   - Use **camelCase** for variables and functions.
   - Keep names concise yet descriptive.

---

3. **Comment Where Necessary** Write comments to explain **why** the code exists, not **what** it does (the code itself should be self-explanatory).
Example:
go
Copy
```go
// calculateTotal adds a discount to the price and returns the final total.
```

113

```go
func calculateTotal(price, discount int) int {

    return price - discount

}
```

Avoid over-commenting obvious code:

go

Copy

```go
// BAD

i := 0 // Initialize variable i to 0
```

4. Organize Code Logically Group related functions and types within the same package or file. For larger projects, create meaningful directories to keep things modular.

Example directory structure:

go

Copy

```
project/

├── models/

│   └── user.go

├── services/

│   └── user_service.go

├── main.go
```

Follow Go's Formatting Standards Use gofmt to automatically format your code and ensure consistency across your project.

sh

Copy

```
gofmt -w .
```

Write Tests Testing ensures maintainability by catching regressions and clarifying the intended behavior of your code.

- o Use the testing package to write unit tests.

Structure your tests alongside your code for clarity:

go

Copy

```
├── service.go

├── service_test.go
```

Example:

go

Copy

```go
func TestCalculateTotal(t *testing.T) {

    result := calculateTotal(100, 20)

    if result != 80 {

        t.Errorf("Expected 80, got %d", result)

    }

}
```

Anti-Patterns to Avoid

Magic Numbers Avoid hardcoding numbers or strings without context.

go

Copy

```
// BAD

const pi = 3.14159
```

Better: Use descriptive constants:

go

Copy

```
const CircleRatio = 3.14159
```

1. **Overcomplicating Error Handling** Keep error-handling logic simple and clear:

   go

   Copy

   ```
   if err != nil {

   return fmt.Errorf("operation failed: %w", err)

   }
   ```

2. **Deep Nesting** Refactor nested code for clarity:

   go

   Copy

   ```
   // BAD

   if condition1 {

   if condition2 {

   // logic

   }
   ```

```
}
```

```
// BETTER

if !condition1 || !condition2 {

    return

}

// logic
```

By adhering to these principles, your code will remain clear, maintainable, and collaborative over time.

5.4 Structuring Monorepos and Microservices in Go

As projects grow, choosing the right structure becomes critical. Whether you're managing a **monorepo** (single repository for multiple projects) or a **microservice-based architecture** (independent, small services), Go provides flexible tools to handle both.

Monorepos in Go

A monorepo is a single repository containing the code for multiple applications or services. This approach simplifies code sharing and version management but requires careful organization to avoid chaos.

Example Monorepo Structure:

go

Copy

```
monorepo/
├── go.mod
├── services/
│   ├── auth/
│   │   ├── go.mod
│   │   ├── main.go
│   ├── payments/
│   │   ├── go.mod
│   │   ├── main.go
├── shared/
│   ├── models/
│   │   ├── user.go
│   ├── utils/
│   │   ├── math.go
```

Key Practices for Monorepos:

1. **Use Go Modules for Subprojects** Each service or project should have its own go.mod file, allowing independent dependency management.

Example:

sh

Copy

```
cd services/auth

go mod init github.com/username/monorepo/services/auth
```

   o **Centralize Shared Code** Place reusable models and utilities in a shared directory:

   go

   Copy

```
// shared/models/user.go

package models

type User struct {

    ID    int

    Name  string

    Email string

}
```

Import shared code in services:

go

Copy

```
import "github.com/username/monorepo/shared/models"
```

2. **Testing and CI for Monorepos** Use tools like go test ./... to run tests across all services and ensure consistency.
3. **Avoid Tight Coupling** While monorepos encourage code sharing, ensure services are loosely coupled and can operate independently.

Microservices in Go

Microservices involve splitting applications into smaller, independent services that communicate over APIs or messaging systems. Each service is self-contained, with its own database and dependencies.

Example Microservice Structure:

go

Copy

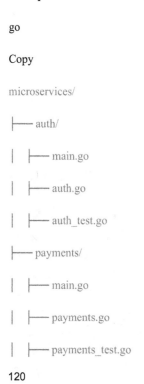

```
microservices/
├── auth/
│   ├── main.go
│   ├── auth.go
│   ├── auth_test.go
├── payments/
│   ├── main.go
│   ├── payments.go
│   ├── payments_test.go
```

Best Practices for Microservices

1. **Use REST or gRPC for Communication**
   - ○ REST: Simple, lightweight, and widely supported.
   - ○ gRPC: High performance and suitable for internal communication.

Example of a REST handler:

go

Copy

```go
func handler(w http.ResponseWriter, r *http.Request) {

  w.WriteHeader(http.StatusOK)

  w.Write([]byte("Hello from Auth Service"))

}
```

2. **Isolate Dependencies** Each service should have its own go.mod file and manage dependencies independently.
3. **Separate Databases** Services should use their own databases to avoid coupling.

Containerize Services Use Docker to containerize each service, ensuring consistent environments across development and production.

Example Dockerfile:

dockerfile

Copy

```dockerfile
FROM golang:1.20

WORKDIR /app

COPY . .
```

```
RUN go build -o main .

CMD ["./main"]
```

4. **Monitor and Log** Use tools like Prometheus and Grafana for monitoring and structured logging libraries (e.g., zap) for detailed insights.

Monorepos vs. Microservices: Choosing the Right Approach

Feature	Monorepo	Microservices
Code Sharing	Easy to share code across projects	Requires duplication or shared libraries
Dependency Mgmt	Centralized with Go modules	Decentralized (each service has its own)
Scalability	Scales with good structure	High scalability, independent deployment
Complexity	Simpler setup, harder to decouple	Requires more tooling for orchestration

---

By structuring monorepos and microservices effectively, Go developers can create scalable, maintainable applications that adapt to the needs of modern development. Choosing the right structure depends on your team size, project complexity, and deployment requirements.

Chapter 6: Testing in Go

Testing is a critical part of software development, ensuring code behaves as expected, remains reliable, and can be refactored with confidence. Go's built-in testing package provides powerful yet straightforward tools for writing tests, making it easy to validate code functionality and catch regressions.

6.1 Introduction to Go's testing Package

The testing package is Go's built-in framework for writing and running tests. It integrates seamlessly with the Go toolchain, requiring minimal setup to get started.

Getting Started With Testing in Go

1. **Creating a Test File**
   - Test files follow the convention *_test.go.
   - Place them alongside the code being tested. Example:

```go
Copy
mypackage/

├── math.go

├── math_test.go
```

2. **Writing a Test Function**
   - Test functions must:
     - Be exported (start with an uppercase Test).

- Take a single *testing.T parameter.
- Have no return values. Example:

go
Copy
```go
package mypackage


func Add(a, b int) int {

    return a + b

}
```

go
Copy
```go
package mypackage

import "testing"

func TestAdd(t *testing.T) {

    result := Add(2, 3)

    if result != 5 {

        t.Errorf("Add(2, 3) = %d; want 5", result)

    }

}
```

Running Tests

Run all tests in a package using the go test command:

sh

Copy

```
go test
```

To see detailed output:

sh

Copy

```
go test -v
```

- To run specific test files:

    sh

    Copy

    ```
    go test -run TestAdd
    ```

Assertions in Go

Unlike many testing frameworks, Go does not provide a built-in assertion library. Instead, use simple conditionals like if to validate test outcomes.

Example:

go

Copy

```
if got != expected {

    t.Errorf("got %d, want %d", got, expected)
```

```
}
```

This explicit style keeps tests simple and clear, while avoiding unnecessary dependencies.

Failing a Test

If a test condition fails, you can signal failure using:

1. **t.Errorf or t.Fatalf**
   - t.Errorf: Reports a test failure but allows the test to continue.
   - t.Fatalf: Reports a failure and immediately stops the test.
2. **t.Fail or t.FailNow**
   - t.Fail: Marks the test as failed but continues execution.
   - t.FailNow: Stops execution immediately.

Skipping Tests

Use t.Skip to skip tests dynamically.

go

Copy

```go
func TestExample(t *testing.T) {

    if testing.Short() {

        t.Skip("skipping test in short mode")

    }
}
```

```
    // Test logic here

}
```

Run tests in short mode:

sh

Copy

```
go test -short
```

Benchmarks

The testing package also supports benchmarks to measure performance. Benchmark functions:

- Start with Benchmark.
- Take a *testing.B parameter.

Example:

go

Copy

```
func BenchmarkAdd(b *testing.B) {

  for i := 0; i < b.N; i++ {

    Add(2, 3)

  }

}
```

127

Run benchmarks:

sh

Copy

```
go test -bench=.
```

Benefits of Using Go's testing Package

1. **Built-In Integration**: No third-party dependencies required.
2. **Simplicity**: The framework is minimal and easy to learn.
3. **Flexibility**: Supports unit tests, benchmarks, and property-based tests.

6.2 Writing Table-Driven Tests

Table-driven tests are a common and idiomatic way of testing in Go. This approach organizes multiple test cases into a single test function, making it easy to add new scenarios and ensure consistency.

What Are Table-Driven Tests?

In table-driven testing, test cases are defined in a slice or array of structs, where each struct represents a single test case with its inputs and expected output.

128

Basic Structure of Table-Driven Tests

1. **Define Test Cases** Create a slice of test cases, where each case contains inputs and expected results.
2. **Iterate Over Test Cases** Use a for loop to execute each test case.
3. **Report Failures** Compare the actual result with the expected result and report any mismatches using t.Errorf.

Example: Table-Driven Test for Addition Function

go

Copy

```go
package mypackage

import "testing"

func Add(a, b int) int {

    return a + b

}

func TestAdd(t *testing.T) {

    // Define test cases

    testCases := []struct {

        name     string

        a, b     int

        expected int
```

```go
}{
    {"both positive", 2, 3, 5},

    {"positive and zero", 5, 0, 5},

    {"both negative", -2, -3, -5},

    {"positive and negative", 5, -3, 2},

}
// Iterate over test cases

for _, tc := range testCases {

    t.Run(tc.name, func(t *testing.T) {

        result := Add(tc.a, tc.b)

        if result != tc.expected {

            t.Errorf("Add(%d, %d) = %d; want %d", tc.a, tc.b, result, tc.expected)

        }

    })

}

}
```

Key Points:

- The t.Run function creates a subtest for each case, providing clearer test output.
- The name field in the struct gives a descriptive name to each test case.

130

Benefits of Table-Driven Tests

1. **Reduced Redundancy**
   - Instead of writing separate test functions for each case, you define all cases in a single table.

2. **Scalability**
   - Adding new test cases is as simple as appending to the table.

3. **Improved Readability**
   - Grouping test cases together makes it easier to understand the scenarios being tested.

Advanced Table-Driven Test Example

For functions with multiple return values or errors, include these in the test case struct.

Example: Testing Division With Error Handling

go

Copy

```
package mypackage

import (

  "errors"

  "testing"

)
```

```go
func Divide(a, b int) (int, error) {

    if b == 0 {

        return 0, errors.New("division by zero")

    }

    return a / b, nil

}

func TestDivide(t *testing.T) {

    // Define test cases

    testCases := []struct {

        name        string

        a, b        int

        expected    int

        expectedError error

    }{

        {"valid division", 10, 2, 5, nil},

        {"division by zero", 10, 0, 0, errors.New("division by zero")},

        {"negative division", -10, 2, -5, nil},

    }
```

```
// Iterate over test cases

for _, tc := range testCases {

    t.Run(tc.name, func(t *testing.T) {

        result, err := Divide(tc.a, tc.b)

        if result != tc.expected || (err != nil && err.Error() != tc.expectedError.Error())) {

            t.Errorf("Divide(%d, %d) = (%d, %v); want (%d, %v)",

                tc.a, tc.b, result, err, tc.expected, tc.expectedError)

        }

    })

}

}
```

Key Considerations:

- Handle both the result and the error in the test logic.
- Use err.Error() to compare error messages if error values are non-nil.

Best Practices for Table-Driven Tests

1. **Use Descriptive Test Names**
   - The name field in each test case provides context about what is being tested.

2. **Minimize Logic in Test Cases**
   - Test cases should focus on inputs and expected results, avoiding unnecessary complexity.
3. **Leverage Subtests**
   - Use t.Run to isolate each test case and provide clear test output.
4. **Keep Tables Focused**
   - Avoid combining unrelated test cases into a single table. Each table should test one function or behavior.

By leveraging Go's testing package and adopting table-driven testing, developers can write concise, readable, and scalable test suites. These tools and patterns help ensure code quality and reduce the risk of regressions, even as projects grow in complexity.

6.3 Test-Driven Development (TDD) With Go

Test-Driven Development (TDD) is a software development methodology that emphasizes writing tests before writing the actual implementation. It follows a cycle of **Red-Green-Refactor**, ensuring code is written to meet specific requirements while maintaining quality.

The TDD Workflow

1. **Red**: Write a failing test that defines the desired behavior or functionality.
2. **Green**: Write the minimal code required to make the test pass.
3. **Refactor**: Clean up the code while ensuring the test still passes.

Benefits of TDD

1. **Early Bug Detection**: Writing tests first forces developers to think through potential edge cases and logic errors.
2. **Improved Code Quality**: Encourages writing modular and testable code.
3. **Clear Requirements**: Tests act as documentation, specifying what the code is expected to do.

TDD in Go: An Example

Let's use TDD to implement a function that calculates the factorial of a number.

Step 1: Write a Failing Test Create the test before implementing the function:

go

Copy

```go
package mypackage

import "testing"

func TestFactorial(t *testing.T) {

  cases := []struct {

    name    string

    input   int

    expected int

  }{

    {"factorial of 0", 0, 1},
```

```go
        {"factorial of 1", 1, 1},

        {"factorial of 5", 5, 120},

    }

    for _, tc := range cases {

        t.Run(tc.name, func(t *testing.T) {

            result := Factorial(tc.input)

            if result != tc.expected {

                t.Errorf("Factorial(%d) = %d; want %d", tc.input, result, tc.expected)

            }

        })

    }

}
```

Since the Factorial function doesn't exist yet, the test will fail.

Step 2: Write Minimal Code to Pass the Test Implement the Factorial function:

go

Copy

```
package mypackage
```

```go
func Factorial(n int) int {

    if n == 0 {

        return 1

    }

    return n * Factorial(n-1)

}
```

Run the test:

sh

Copy

```sh
go test
```

All tests should now pass.

Step 3: Refactor Refactor the function to improve readability or performance while ensuring the tests still pass.

Example:

go

Copy

```go
func Factorial(n int) int {

    result := 1
```

137

```
for i := 1; i <= n; i++ {

    result *= i

}

return result

}
```

By following TDD, you ensure the function meets the requirements, handles edge cases, and remains maintainable.

Best Practices for TDD in Go

1. Write small, focused tests for individual behaviors.
2. Use table-driven tests to cover multiple scenarios efficiently.
3. Avoid skipping the refactor step; always clean up the implementation.
4. Let the test suite guide the design of your code.

6.4 Mocking and Dependency Injection in Tests

When testing code that depends on external systems (e.g., databases, APIs), it's often impractical to use the actual dependencies in tests. Instead, you can use **mocking** and **dependency injection** to isolate the code under test.

Mocking in Go

Mocking involves creating fake implementations of dependencies to simulate behavior during tests. Go's interfaces make it easy to define and substitute mocks.

138

Example: Mocking a Service

Suppose you have a service that depends on a database:

go

Copy

```go
type Database interface {

    GetUser(id int) (string, error)

}

type UserService struct {

    DB Database

}

func (s *UserService) GetUserName(id int) (string, error) {

    return s.DB.GetUser(id)

}
```

Mock Implementation:

go

Copy

```go
type MockDatabase struct{}
```

```go
func (m *MockDatabase) GetUser(id int) (string, error) {

    if id == 1 {

        return "Alice", nil

    }

    return "", fmt.Errorf("user not found")

}
```

Test Using the Mock:

go

Copy

```go
func TestGetUserName(t *testing.T) {

    mockDB := &MockDatabase{}

    service := UserService{DB: mockDB}

    name, err := service.GetUserName(1)

    if err != nil || name != "Alice" {

        t.Errorf("expected Alice, got %s (err: %v)", name, err)

    }

}
```

Dependency Injection

Dependency injection is a design pattern where dependencies are passed into a component instead of being created inside it. This makes the component easier to test and more flexible.

Example: Injecting a Database Dependency

go

Copy

```go
func NewUserService(db Database) *UserService {

    return &UserService{DB: db}

}

func TestUserService(t *testing.T) {

    mockDB := &MockDatabase{}

    service := NewUserService(mockDB)

    // Test logic here

}
```

Benefits of Dependency Injection:

1. Simplifies testing by allowing you to swap real dependencies with mocks.
2. Reduces coupling, making the code more modular.

6.5 Profiling and Benchmarking Your Code

Performance is critical for many applications. Go provides built-in tools for profiling and benchmarking to help identify bottlenecks and optimize code.

Profiling in Go

Profiling helps measure CPU, memory, and other resource usage to identify inefficient code. The pprof package provides tools for this purpose.

CPU Profiling Example:

go

Copy

```go
package main

import (

    "os"

    "runtime/pprof"

)

func main() {

    f, _ := os.Create("cpu.prof")

    pprof.StartCPUProfile(f)

    defer pprof.StopCPUProfile()
```

```
// Code to profile

for i := 0; i < 1000000; i++ {

    _ = i * i

  }

}
```

Run the profiling code and analyze the results:

sh

Copy

```
go run main.go

go tool pprof cpu.prof
```

Common Commands in pprof:

- top: Shows the functions consuming the most CPU.
- list [function]: Displays detailed profiling data for a specific function.

Memory Profiling Example:

go

Copy

```
package main
```

```go
import (

    "os"

    "runtime/pprof"

)

func main() {

    f, _ := os.Create("mem.prof")

    pprof.WriteHeapProfile(f)

    defer f.Close()

    // Simulate memory allocation

    data := make([]int, 1000000)

    _ = data

}
```

Analyze the memory profile:

sh

Copy

```sh
go tool pprof mem.prof
```

Benchmarking in Go

Benchmarking measures the performance of specific functions. Benchmark functions:

1. Start with Benchmark.
2. Take a *testing.B parameter.
3. Use b.N to control the number of iterations.

Example:

go

Copy

```
package mypackage

import "testing"

func Add(a, b int) int {

  return a + b

}

func BenchmarkAdd(b *testing.B) {

  for i := 0; i < b.N; i++ {

    Add(2, 3)

  }

}
```

Run benchmarks:

sh

Copy

```
go test -bench=.
```

Tips for Effective Benchmarking

1. **Avoid Logging in Benchmarks** Logging can distort benchmark results by introducing I/O overhead.
2. **Isolate Code** Benchmark only the specific functionality you want to measure.
3. **Compare Performance Before and After Changes** Use benchmarks to evaluate the impact of optimizations.

Use -benchmem Include memory allocations in benchmark output:
sh
Copy
```
go test -bench=. -benchmem
```

Best Practices for Profiling and Benchmarking

1. **Profile in Realistic Scenarios** Run your application under realistic workloads to get meaningful profiling data.
2. **Optimize Bottlenecks** Focus on areas where most CPU or memory resources are consumed.
3. **Use Visualization Tools** Tools like pprof's web interface or third-party tools (e.g., GoLand) can make profiling data easier to understand.

4. **Balance Optimization** Avoid premature optimization. Profile your application first to ensure changes target real bottlenecks.

By incorporating TDD, mocking, dependency injection, and performance measurement into your workflow, you can create robust, testable, and high-performing Go applications. These practices help ensure your code meets both functional and performance expectations.

Chapter 7: Advanced Idioms and Patterns

As you gain more experience with Go, understanding advanced idioms and patterns becomes essential for writing efficient, idiomatic, and maintainable code. This chapter explores ways to avoid common pitfalls (anti-patterns) and introduces advanced concurrency techniques to build robust applications.

7.1 Avoiding Common Go Anti-Patterns

Even though Go promotes simplicity, developers sometimes fall into traps that can lead to inefficient or unmaintainable code. Recognizing and avoiding these anti-patterns ensures your code remains clean and idiomatic.

---

1. Overusing Goroutines

Problem: Launching too many goroutines without considering resource limitations can lead to high memory usage and unexpected behavior.

Example (Anti-Pattern):

go

Copy

```
for i := 0; i < 1000000; i++ {

    go process(i) // Creates one million goroutines

}
```

148

Solution: Use a worker pool to limit the number of concurrent goroutines.

go

Copy

```go
func process(id int) {

    // Processing logic here

}

func main() {

    tasks := make(chan int, 100)

    for i := 0; i < 10; i++ {

        go func() {

            for task := range tasks {

                process(task)

            }

        }()

    }

    for i := 0; i < 1000; i++ {

        tasks <- i

    }
```

```
close(tasks)
```

```
}
```

---

2. Ignoring Errors

Problem: Skipping error handling can lead to unpredictable program behavior and hidden bugs.

Example (Anti-Pattern):

go

Copy

```go
file, _ := os.Open("config.json") // Error is ignored
```

Solution: Always handle errors, even if it's just logging them.

go

Copy

```go
file, err := os.Open("config.json")

if err != nil {

    log.Fatalf("Failed to open file: %v", err)

}

defer file.Close()
```

3. Overcomplicating Interfaces

Problem: Defining overly large or generic interfaces makes it harder to implement and test code.

Example (Anti-Pattern):

go

Copy

```
type DataStore interface {

    Read() ([]byte, error)

    Write([]byte) error

    Delete() error

    List() ([]string, error)

    Backup() error

}
```

Solution: Break down large interfaces into smaller, focused ones.

go

Copy

```
type Reader interface {

    Read() ([]byte, error)
```

```go
}

type Writer interface {

    Write([]byte) error

}
```

---

4. Deep Nesting

Problem: Excessive nesting makes code harder to read and maintain.

Example (Anti-Pattern):

go

Copy

```go
if condition1 {

    if condition2 {

        if condition3 {

            // Deeply nested logic

        }

    }

}
```

Solution: Refactor nested code with early returns or helper functions.

go

Copy

```
if !condition1 || !condition2 || !condition3 {

    return

}
```

// Logic here

---

5. Premature Optimization

Problem: Optimizing code without understanding actual performance bottlenecks wastes time and can make the code harder to understand.

Example (Anti-Pattern):

go

Copy

// Using low-level hacks to avoid allocations prematurely

Solution: Profile your application first to identify real bottlenecks using tools like pprof. Optimize only where necessary.

---

6. Re-inventing the Wheel

Problem: Writing custom solutions for features that are already part of Go's standard library.

Example (Anti-Pattern):

go

Copy

// Writing a custom HTTP server when net/http is sufficient

Solution: Use Go's built-in tools and libraries whenever possible. For example, use sync.WaitGroup for goroutine synchronization instead of writing your own.

7.2 Advanced Concurrency Patterns

Go's concurrency model is a powerful tool for building efficient, scalable systems. While goroutines and channels are simple to use, mastering advanced patterns helps you tackle more complex scenarios.

---

1. Worker Pool

A worker pool limits the number of goroutines processing tasks, ensuring controlled resource usage.

Example:

go

Copy

package main

```go
import (

    "fmt"

    "sync"

)

func worker(id int, tasks <-chan int, wg *sync.WaitGroup) {

    defer wg.Done()

    for task := range tasks {

        fmt.Printf("Worker %d processing task %d\n", id, task)

    }

}

func main() {

    tasks := make(chan int, 10)

    var wg sync.WaitGroup

    // Start worker goroutines

    for i := 1; i <= 3; i++ {

        wg.Add(1)

        go worker(i, tasks, &wg)

    }
```

```go
// Send tasks to the workers

for i := 1; i <= 10; i++ {

    tasks <- i

}

close(tasks) // Signal workers to stop when all tasks are processed

wg.Wait() // Wait for all workers to finish

fmt.Println("All tasks completed")

}
```

---

2. Fan-Out and Fan-In

- **Fan-Out**: Distribute tasks to multiple goroutines for parallel processing.
- **Fan-In**: Collect results from multiple goroutines into a single channel.

Example:

go

Copy

```go
package main

import "fmt"

func fanOut(tasks []int) <-chan int {

    output := make(chan int)
```

```go
    go func() {

        for _, task := range tasks {

            output <- task

        }

        close(output)

    }()

    return output

}

func worker(input <-chan int) <-chan int {

    output := make(chan int)

    go func() {

        for task := range input {

            output <- task * 2 // Process task

        }

        close(output)

    }()

    return output

}
```

```go
func fanIn(inputs ...<-chan int) <-chan int {

    output := make(chan int)

    var wg sync.WaitGroup

    wg.Add(len(inputs))

    for _, ch := range inputs {

        go func(c <-chan int) {

            for value := range c {

                output <- value

            }

            wg.Done()

        }(ch)

    }

    go func() {

        wg.Wait()

        close(output)

    }()

    return output

}

func main() {
```

```go
tasks := []int{1, 2, 3, 4, 5}

input := fanOut(tasks)

worker1 := worker(input)

worker2 := worker(input)

results := fanIn(worker1, worker2)

for result := range results {

    fmt.Println("Result:", result)

}

}
```

---

3. Pipelines

Pipelines allow data to flow through multiple stages, with each stage running concurrently.

Example:

go

Copy

```go
package main

import "fmt"
```

```go
func stage1(input []int) <-chan int {

    output := make(chan int)

    go func() {

        for _, num := range input {

            output <- num * 2

        }

        close(output)

    }()

    return output

}

func stage2(input <-chan int) <-chan int {

    output := make(chan int)

    go func() {

        for num := range input {

            output <- num + 1

        }

        close(output)

    }()

    return output
```

```go
}

func main() {
    input := []int{1, 2, 3, 4, 5}

    result := stage2(stage1(input))

    for val := range result {

        fmt.Println("Result:", val)

    }

}
```

---

4. Rate Limiting

Rate limiting ensures that operations occur at a controlled pace.

Example Using time.Ticker:

go

Copy

```go
package main

import (

    "fmt"

    "time"
```

```go
)

func main() {

    ticker := time.NewTicker(500 * time.Millisecond)

    defer ticker.Stop()


    for i := 0; i < 5; i++ {

        <-ticker.C

        fmt.Printf("Task %d executed at %s\n", i, time.Now())

    }

}
```

---

5. Using Select With Channels

The select statement allows a goroutine to wait on multiple channel operations, enabling complex synchronization patterns.

Example:

go

Copy

```go
package main
```

```go
import (

    "fmt"

    "time"

)

func main() {

    ch1 := make(chan string)

    ch2 := make(chan string)

    go func() {

        time.Sleep(1 * time.Second)

        ch1 <- "Message from ch1"

    }()

    go func() {

        time.Sleep(2 * time.Second)

        ch2 <- "Message from ch2"

    }()

    for i := 0; i < 2; i++ {

        select {

        case msg1 := <-ch1:

            fmt.Println(msg1)
```

```
    case msg2 := <-ch2:

        fmt.Println(msg2)

    }

  }

}
```

By avoiding anti-patterns and mastering advanced concurrency patterns, Go developers can write scalable, efficient, and idiomatic applications. These practices ensure your code remains robust under high load and complex real-world scenarios.

7.3 Leveraging Reflection in Go (With Caution)

Reflection in Go allows programs to inspect and manipulate their own structure at runtime. While it can be incredibly powerful, reflection should be used sparingly due to its complexity and potential performance overhead.

What Is Reflection in Go?

Reflection is enabled by the reflect package, which provides tools to examine types, values, and interfaces at runtime.

Key components:

1. reflect.Type: Represents the type of a value.
2. reflect.Value: Represents the value of a variable, including the ability to modify it.
3. reflect.Interface: Converts a reflect.Value back to an interface.

Basic Example of Reflection

go

Copy

```go
package main

import (
    "fmt"
    "reflect"
)

func main() {
    var x int = 42
    t := reflect.TypeOf(x) // Get type information
    v := reflect.ValueOf(x) // Get value information
    fmt.Println("Type:", t)      // Output: int
    fmt.Println("Value:", v)    // Output: 42
    fmt.Println("Kind:", t.Kind()) // Output: int (kind refers to the base type)
}
```

Use Cases for Reflection

Inspecting Struct Fields

go

Copy

```go
type Person struct {

    Name string

    Age  int

}

func printStructFields(s interface{}) {

    t := reflect.TypeOf(s)

    v := reflect.ValueOf(s)

    for i := 0; i < t.NumField(); i++ {

        field := t.Field(i)

        value := v.Field(i)

        fmt.Printf("Field: %s, Value: %v\n", field.Name, value)

    }

}

func main() {

    p := Person{Name: "Alice", Age: 30}

    printStructFields(p)
```

}

1. Dynamic Function Calls

go

Copy

```go
func add(a, b int) int {

    return a + b

}

func callDynamic(fn interface{}, args ...interface{}) interface{} {

    f := reflect.ValueOf(fn)

    inputs := make([]reflect.Value, len(args))

    for i, arg := range args {

        inputs[i] = reflect.ValueOf(arg)

    }

    results := f.Call(inputs)

    return results[0].Interface()

}

func main() {

    result := callDynamic(add, 2, 3)

    fmt.Println("Result:", result) // Output: 5

}
```

Cautions With Reflection

1. **Performance Overhead** Reflection is slower than regular code because it bypasses compile-time type checking and involves runtime computation.
2. **Complexity** Reflective code is harder to read, maintain, and debug.
3. **Use Cases to Avoid**
   - Replacing straightforward implementations with reflection.
   - Excessive use of reflection in performance-critical sections.

Best Practice: Use reflection only when you cannot solve a problem cleanly with static typing.

7.4 Using Functional Options for API Design

Functional options are a flexible and idiomatic design pattern in Go for creating APIs with configurable behavior. They allow you to provide optional parameters to functions or constructors in a clean and readable way.

Why Use Functional Options?

1. **Avoids Parameter Explosion** Functions or constructors with many parameters can become unwieldy, especially when most of the parameters are optional.
2. **Improves Readability** Callers can specify only the options they care about, resulting in cleaner code.
3. **Extensibility** New options can be added without breaking existing code.

Basic Example of Functional Options

Without Functional Options:

go

Copy

```
type Server struct {
    Port    int
    Timeout int
}


func NewServer(port, timeout int) *Server {
    return &Server{Port: port, Timeout: timeout}
}


func main() {
    s := NewServer(8080, 30) // Hard to know what 8080 and 30 represent
    fmt.Println(s)
}
```

With Functional Options:

169

go

Copy

```go
type Server struct {

    Port    int

    Timeout int

}


type Option func(*Server)


func WithPort(port int) Option {

    return func(s *Server) {

        s.Port = port

    }

}


func WithTimeout(timeout int) Option {

    return func(s *Server) {

        s.Timeout = timeout

    }
```

```go
}


func NewServer(opts ...Option) *Server {

    s := &Server{Port: 80, Timeout: 60} // Default values

    for _, opt := range opts {

        opt(s)

    }

    return s

}


func main() {

    s := NewServer(WithPort(8080), WithTimeout(30))

    fmt.Printf("Server: %+v\n", s)

}
```

Advantages of Functional Options

1. **Default Values** Default values are set within the constructor, and options override them selectively.
2. **Readability** The intent of each option is clear in the calling code.
3. **Extensibility** Adding a new option is as simple as creating a new Option function.

Best Practices for Functional Options

1. Use meaningful names for option functions.
2. Combine functional options with immutability principles where possible.
3. Document default values clearly.

7.5 The Power of context: Advanced Usage

The context package provides a standard way to manage request-scoped data, deadlines, and cancellation signals in concurrent applications.

Review of context Basics

- **Creating Contexts**
    - context.Background(): The root context, used for top-level contexts.
    - context.WithCancel(): Creates a cancellable context.
    - context.WithTimeout(): Adds a timeout to a context.

Basic Example:

go

Copy

```
ctx, cancel := context.WithTimeout(context.Background(), 2*time.Second)

defer cancel()
```

```go
select {

case <-time.After(3 * time.Second):

    fmt.Println("Operation timed out")

case <-ctx.Done():

    fmt.Println("Context canceled:", ctx.Err())

}
```

Advanced context Use Cases

Propagating Context in API Calls Pass context to functions to ensure deadlines and cancellations propagate correctly.

go
Copy
```go
func fetchData(ctx context.Context) error {

  select {

  case <-time.After(3 * time.Second):

    return nil // Simulate data fetching

  case <-ctx.Done():

    return ctx.Err() // Handle context cancellation

  }

}
```

173

```go
func main() {

    ctx, cancel := context.WithTimeout(context.Background(), 2*time.Second)

    defer cancel()


    if err := fetchData(ctx); err != nil {

        fmt.Println("Error:", err)

    }

}
```

1. **Using Context for Per-Request Values** Store and retrieve request-scoped data using context.WithValue.

    go

    Copy

```go
    func logRequest(ctx context.Context) {

userID := ctx.Value("userID").(int)

fmt.Printf("Handling request for user %d\n", userID)

}

func main() {

    ctx := context.WithValue(context.Background(), "userID", 123)

    logRequest(ctx)

}
```

2. **Caution:** Avoid using context.WithValue for passing non-essential data. Use explicit parameters where possible.

Combining Contexts With Goroutines Cancel goroutines gracefully when the context is canceled.

go

Copy

```go
func worker(ctx context.Context) {

    for {

        select {

        case <-ctx.Done():

            fmt.Println("Worker stopped:", ctx.Err())

            return

        default:

            fmt.Println("Worker running")

            time.Sleep(500 * time.Millisecond)

        }

    }

}


func main() {

    ctx, cancel := context.WithTimeout(context.Background(), 2*time.Second)
```

```go
    defer cancel()

    go worker(ctx)

    time.Sleep(3 * time.Second)
}
```

Best Practices for context

Always pass context as the first argument to functions.

go

Copy

```go
func process(ctx context.Context, data string) error {

    // Function logic

}
```

1. Use meaningful keys when using context.WithValue. Prefer defining custom types for keys to avoid collisions.
2. Avoid storing large data structures in the context.

Always cancel contexts you create to release resources:

go

Copy

```go
ctx, cancel := context.WithTimeout(context.Background(), 5*time.Second)

defer cancel()
```

3. Test context behavior using real-world scenarios like timeouts and cancellations to ensure robustness.

By leveraging reflection sparingly, adopting functional options for flexible APIs, and mastering advanced context usage, you can write highly scalable and maintainable Go applications. These patterns and idioms help tackle complex requirements while keeping your code idiomatic and clean.

Chapter 8: Performance Optimization

Optimizing performance is a key aspect of building robust and efficient applications. Go provides a suite of tools and features, including profiling utilities and garbage collection management, to help identify bottlenecks and optimize resource usage.

8.1 Profiling Tools: pprof and benchstat

Profiling tools are essential for identifying CPU and memory usage, pinpointing inefficient code, and guiding optimizations.

Using pprof for Profiling

The pprof package is Go's built-in tool for analyzing application performance. It supports profiling CPU usage, memory allocation, goroutines, and more.

CPU Profiling

Steps:

1. Import the runtime/pprof package.
2. Use StartCPUProfile and StopCPUProfile to generate a CPU profile.

Example:

go

Copy

```go
package main

import (
    "os"
    "runtime/pprof"
    "time"
)

func main() {
    f, err := os.Create("cpu.prof")
    if err != nil {
        panic(err)
    }
    defer f.Close()

    pprof.StartCPUProfile(f)
    defer pprof.StopCPUProfile()

    simulateWork()
```

```go
}


func simulateWork() {

  for i := 0; i < 1_000_000; i++ {

    _ = i * i

  }

  time.Sleep(1 * time.Second)

}
```

Analyze the Profile: After generating cpu.prof, analyze it using the pprof tool:

sh

Copy

```sh
go tool pprof cpu.prof
```

Key commands:

- top: Lists the most CPU-intensive functions.
- list [function_name]: Shows detailed profiling data for a specific function.
- web: Opens an interactive graph in your browser (requires Graphviz).

Memory Profiling

Steps:

1. Use WriteHeapProfile to capture memory usage.

Example:

go

Copy

```go
package main

import (
    "os"
    "runtime/pprof"
)

func main() {
    f, err := os.Create("mem.prof")
    if err != nil {
        panic(err)
    }
    defer f.Close()
```

```go
    data := make([]byte, 100_000_000) // Simulate memory allocation
    _ = data


    pprof.WriteHeapProfile(f)
}
```

Analyze Memory Profile:

sh

Copy

```sh
go tool pprof mem.prof
```

Using net/http/pprof for Profiling in Web Applications

For web servers, the net/http/pprof package provides an easy way to add runtime profiling endpoints.

Example:

go

Copy

182

```go
package main

import (
    _ "net/http/pprof"
    "net/http"
)

func main() {
    go simulateWork()
    http.ListenAndServe(":6060", nil) // Access profiling data at
localhost:6060/debug/pprof/
}

func simulateWork() {
    for {
        _ = make([]byte, 1_000_000) // Simulate memory allocations
    }
}
```

Visit http://localhost:6060/debug/pprof/ to access profiling data.

Using benchstat for Benchmark Analysis

benchstat is a tool for comparing benchmark results, useful for evaluating performance improvements after code changes.

Write benchmarks using Go's testing package:
go
Copy
```
func BenchmarkAddition(b *testing.B) {

  for i := 0; i < b.N; i++ {

    _ = 1 + 1

  }

}
```

1. Run benchmarks and save results:
   sh
   Copy
   ```
   go test -bench=. > old.txt
   ```

2. Modify the code and run benchmarks again:
   sh
   Copy
   ```
   go test -bench=. > new.txt
   ```

3. Compare results using benchstat:

sh

Copy

```
benchstat old.txt new.txt
```

4. **Output:**

sql

Copy

```
name    old time/op  new time/op  delta
Add     5.12ns ± 3%  4.90ns ± 2%  -4.3%
```

Tips for Effective Profiling

1. Profile in realistic environments to capture real-world performance characteristics.
2. Use pprof output to identify bottlenecks and prioritize optimizations.
3. Combine profiling with benchmarks to measure the impact of changes.

8.2 Memory Management and Garbage Collection

Efficient memory management is crucial for high-performance applications. Go's garbage collector (GC) handles memory cleanup automatically, but understanding its behavior can help you write more efficient code.

How Garbage Collection Works in Go

The garbage collector:

1. Tracks allocated objects.
2. Identifies objects that are no longer referenced.
3. Reclaims memory used by unreachable objects.

Go's GC is optimized for low latency, making it suitable for applications requiring high responsiveness.

Optimizing Memory Usage

Avoid Excessive Allocation Minimize memory allocation by reusing objects where possible.

Example:

go

Copy

```
// Instead of creating a new slice repeatedly:

data := make([]int, 0, 1000)
```

1. **Reduce Object Lifetime** The longer an object stays in memory, the more work the GC has to do. Limit the scope of variables to avoid unnecessary retention.

Use Pooled Objects For frequently used objects, consider using the sync.Pool to reduce allocation overhead.

Example:

go

Copy

```
import "sync"
```

```go
var pool = sync.Pool{

    New: func() interface{} {

        return make([]byte, 1024)

    },

}

func main() {

    buf := pool.Get().([]byte)

    // Use buffer

    pool.Put(buf)

}
```

Analyzing and Reducing Garbage Collection Overhead

Profile Allocation Frequency Use pprof to identify functions responsible for frequent allocations.

Example:
sh
Copy
```
go tool pprof -alloc_space mem.prof
```

1. **Use Escape Analysis** The -gcflags="-m" flag helps identify variables that escape to the heap, which can increase GC pressure.

   Example:

   sh

   Copy

   go build -gcflags="-m" main.go

Output:

css

Copy

main.go:10: moved to heap: x

2. **Optimize Slice Usage** Avoid unnecessary slice growth to minimize reallocation costs.

   Example:

   go

   Copy

   ```
   // BAD: Repeated reallocation

   var nums []int

   for i := 0; i < 1000; i++ {

     nums = append(nums, i)

   }

   // GOOD: Preallocate capacity

   nums := make([]int, 0, 1000)

   for i := 0; i < 1000; i++ {

     nums = append(nums, i)
   ```

188

```
}
```

Garbage Collection Metrics

Monitor GC performance using the runtime package:

go

Copy

```go
package main

import (
    "fmt"
    "runtime"
)

func main() {
    var stats runtime.MemStats
    runtime.ReadMemStats(&stats)
    fmt.Printf("Alloc: %v KB\n", stats.Alloc/1024)
    fmt.Printf("TotalAlloc: %v KB\n", stats.TotalAlloc/1024)
    fmt.Printf("HeapAlloc: %v KB\n", stats.HeapAlloc/1024)
```

```
fmt.Printf("NumGC: %v\n", stats.NumGC)

}
```

When to Tune GC Settings

Use environment variables to adjust GC behavior in specific scenarios:

GOGC: Controls the garbage collection frequency. Higher values reduce GC frequency, while lower values increase it.

sh

Copy

```
GOGC=100 go run main.go
```

1. GODEBUG: Provides detailed GC logging for debugging.

   sh

   Copy

   ```
   GODEBUG=gctrace=1 go run main.go
   ```

Example output:

css

Copy

```
gc 1 @0.005s 0%: 0.015+0.050+0.005 ms
```

Best Practices for Memory Management

1. Profile memory usage before optimizing to identify real issues.
2. Preallocate slices and maps when possible to avoid repeated growth.
3. Use pooling for reusable objects in performance-critical sections.
4. Monitor garbage collection metrics to ensure GC does not become a bottleneck.

By leveraging Go's profiling tools and understanding memory management, you can identify bottlenecks, optimize resource usage, and build efficient applications. These techniques help ensure your code performs well under both typical and heavy workloads.

Chapter 8: Performance Optimization

Optimizing performance is a key aspect of building robust and efficient applications. Go provides a suite of tools and features, including profiling utilities and garbage collection management, to help identify bottlenecks and optimize resource usage.

8.1 Profiling Tools: pprof and benchstat

Profiling tools are essential for identifying CPU and memory usage, pinpointing inefficient code, and guiding optimizations.

Using pprof for Profiling

The pprof package is Go's built-in tool for analyzing application performance. It supports profiling CPU usage, memory allocation, goroutines, and more.

CPU Profiling

Steps:

1. Import the runtime/pprof package.
2. Use StartCPUProfile and StopCPUProfile to generate a CPU profile.

Example:

go

Copy

```go
package main

import (
    "os"
    "runtime/pprof"
    "time"
)

func main() {
    f, err := os.Create("cpu.prof")
    if err != nil {
        panic(err)
    }
    defer f.Close()

    pprof.StartCPUProfile(f)
```

```
    defer pprof.StopCPUProfile()

    simulateWork()
}


func simulateWork() {
    for i := 0; i < 1_000_000; i++ {
        _ = i * i
    }
    time.Sleep(1 * time.Second)
}
```

Analyze the Profile: After generating cpu.prof, analyze it using the pprof tool:

sh

Copy

```
go tool pprof cpu.prof
```

Key commands:

- top: Lists the most CPU-intensive functions.

- list [function_name]: Shows detailed profiling data for a specific function.
- web: Opens an interactive graph in your browser (requires Graphviz).

Memory Profiling

Steps:

1. Use WriteHeapProfile to capture memory usage.

Example:

go

Copy

```go
package main

import (
    "os"
    "runtime/pprof"
)

func main() {
    f, err := os.Create("mem.prof")
    if err != nil {
```

```
    panic(err)

  }

  defer f.Close()


  data := make([]byte, 100_000_000) // Simulate memory allocation

  _ = data


  pprof.WriteHeapProfile(f)

}
```

Analyze Memory Profile:

sh

Copy

```
go tool pprof mem.prof
```

Using net/http/pprof for Profiling in Web Applications

For web servers, the net/http/pprof package provides an easy way to add runtime profiling endpoints.

195

Example:

go

Copy

```go
package main

import (
    _ "net/http/pprof"
    "net/http"
)

func main() {
    go simulateWork()
    http.ListenAndServe(":6060", nil) // Access profiling data at
localhost:6060/debug/pprof/
}

func simulateWork() {
    for {
        _ = make([]byte, 1_000_000) // Simulate memory allocations
```

```
  }

}
```

Visit http://localhost:6060/debug/pprof/ to access profiling data.

Using benchstat for Benchmark Analysis

benchstat is a tool for comparing benchmark results, useful for evaluating performance improvements after code changes.

Write benchmarks using Go's testing package:

go

Copy

```
func BenchmarkAddition(b *testing.B) {

  for i := 0; i < b.N; i++ {

    _ = 1 + 1

  }

}
```

    1.

Run benchmarks and save results:

sh

Copy

```
go test -bench=. > old.txt
```

    2.

Modify the code and run benchmarks again:

sh

Copy

```
go test -bench=. > new.txt
```

3.

Compare results using benchstat:

sh

Copy

```
benchstat old.txt new.txt
```

4.

Output:

sql

Copy

```
name    old time/op  new time/op  delta

Add     5.12ns ± 3%  4.90ns ± 2%  -4.3%
```

Tips for Effective Profiling

1. Profile in realistic environments to capture real-world performance characteristics.
2. Use pprof output to identify bottlenecks and prioritize optimizations.
3. Combine profiling with benchmarks to measure the impact of changes.

198

8.2 Memory Management and Garbage Collection

Efficient memory management is crucial for high-performance applications. Go's garbage collector (GC) handles memory cleanup automatically, but understanding its behavior can help you write more efficient code.

How Garbage Collection Works in Go

The garbage collector:

1. Tracks allocated objects.
2. Identifies objects that are no longer referenced.
3. Reclaims memory used by unreachable objects.

Go's GC is optimized for low latency, making it suitable for applications requiring high responsiveness.

Optimizing Memory Usage

Avoid Excessive Allocation Minimize memory allocation by reusing objects where possible.

Example:

go

Copy

```go
// Instead of creating a new slice repeatedly:

data := make([]int, 0, 1000)
```

1. **Reduce Object Lifetime** The longer an object stays in memory, the more work the GC has to do. Limit the scope of variables to avoid unnecessary retention.

Use Pooled Objects For frequently used objects, consider using the sync.Pool to reduce allocation overhead.

Example:

go

Copy

```go
import "sync"



var pool = sync.Pool{

    New: func() interface{} {

        return make([]byte, 1024)

    },

}



func main() {

    buf := pool.Get().([]byte)

    // Use buffer

    pool.Put(buf)

}
```

Analyzing and Reducing Garbage Collection Overhead

Profile Allocation Frequency Use pprof to identify functions responsible for frequent allocations.

Example:

sh

Copy

```
go tool pprof -alloc_space mem.prof
```

1. **Use Escape Analysis** The -gcflags="-m" flag helps identify variables that escape to the heap, which can increase GC pressure.

   Example:

   sh

   Copy

   ```
   go build -gcflags="-m" main.go
   ```

Output:

css

Copy

```
main.go:10: moved to heap: x
```

2. **Optimize Slice Usage** Avoid unnecessary slice growth to minimize reallocation costs.

   Example:

   go

   Copy

   ```
   // BAD: Repeated reallocation
   ```

```
var nums []int
```

```
for i := 0; i < 1000; i++ {
```

```
    nums = append(nums, i)
```

```
}
```

```
// GOOD: Preallocate capacity

nums := make([]int, 0, 1000)

for i := 0; i < 1000; i++ {

    nums = append(nums, i)

}
```

Garbage Collection Metrics

Monitor GC performance using the runtime package:

go

Copy

```go
package main


import (

    "fmt"

    "runtime"

)
```

```go
func main() {

    var stats runtime.MemStats

    runtime.ReadMemStats(&stats)

    fmt.Printf("Alloc: %v KB\n", stats.Alloc/1024)

    fmt.Printf("TotalAlloc: %v KB\n", stats.TotalAlloc/1024)

    fmt.Printf("HeapAlloc: %v KB\n", stats.HeapAlloc/1024)

    fmt.Printf("NumGC: %v\n", stats.NumGC)

}
```

When to Tune GC Settings

Use environment variables to adjust GC behavior in specific scenarios:

GOGC: Controls the garbage collection frequency. Higher values reduce GC frequency, while lower values increase it.
sh
Copy
```sh
GOGC=100 go run main.go
```

1. **GODEBUG**: Provides detailed GC logging for debugging.
   sh
   Copy
   ```sh
   GODEBUG=gctrace=1 go run main.go
   ```

Example output:

css

Copy

gc 1 @0.005s 0%: 0.015+0.050+0.005 ms

8.3 Writing CPU-Efficient Code

When working with CPU-bound operations, optimizing computation can significantly reduce processing time and improve responsiveness. The key to CPU efficiency often lies in refining algorithms, leveraging concurrency wisely, and minimizing unnecessary work.

Profiling First

Before making changes, use pprof and benchmarks to identify the most CPU-intensive functions. Focus on optimizing hot paths—areas of code where the CPU spends most of its time.

Strategies for CPU Optimization

1. **Choose the Right Algorithm**
   - Replacing an $O(n^2)$ algorithm with an $O(n \log n)$ or $O(n)$ approach can have dramatic effects on performance.
   - For example, sorting large datasets with a more efficient algorithm or using hash-based lookups instead of linear scans.
2. **Reduce Allocations**

- Memory allocations can slow down CPU performance due to increased garbage collection overhead.
- Use preallocated slices, reusable buffers, and object pools to minimize runtime allocations.

Example:

go

Copy

```
// BAD: Allocating inside a loop

for i := 0; i < 1000; i++ {

    data := make([]byte, 1024)

    process(data)

}

// GOOD: Reuse a single buffer

buf := make([]byte, 1024)

for i := 0; i < 1000; i++ {

    process(buf)

}
```

3. **Parallelize Workloads**
   - If the workload is independent (e.g., processing elements in a large dataset), consider splitting it across multiple goroutines to take advantage of multiple CPU cores.

Example:

go

205

Copy

```go
import (

    "runtime"

    "sync"

)



func processChunk(start, end int, data []int, wg *sync.WaitGroup) {

    defer wg.Done()

    for i := start; i < end; i++ {

        data[i] *= 2

    }

}



func main() {

    data := make([]int, 1_000_000)

    numWorkers := runtime.NumCPU()

    chunkSize := len(data) / numWorkers


    var wg sync.WaitGroup
```

```
for i := 0; i < numWorkers; i++ {

    start := i * chunkSize

    end := start + chunkSize

    wg.Add(1)

    go processChunk(start, end, data, &wg)

}

wg.Wait()

}
```

4. **Optimize Critical Loops**
   - Minimize operations inside frequently executed loops.
   - Move invariant calculations outside the loop to avoid repeated work.
5. **Leverage Built-In Functions**
   - Use Go's standard library functions and built-in operations whenever possible. They are highly optimized for performance.
6. **Use the unsafe Package Carefully**
   - In rare cases, the unsafe package can eliminate overhead, but it should be used sparingly and only when performance gains are critical.

Common CPU Pitfalls to Avoid

1. **Excessive Logging**
   - Printing to the console or writing logs can be CPU-intensive. Reduce logging frequency or disable unnecessary logging in performance-critical sections.

2. **Unnecessary Conversions**

    ○ Repeatedly converting between data types (e.g., strings to byte slices and back) can add overhead. Perform conversions once and reuse the result.

3. **Blocking Operations**

    ○ Avoid blocking operations in critical CPU-bound code paths. If blocking is necessary, ensure it doesn't impact overall throughput by parallelizing other work.

Profiling After Optimization

After making changes, re-run benchmarks and pprof to confirm that the changes improved performance. Focus on measurable gains and continue refining until the performance reaches an acceptable level.

8.4 Tips for Optimizing I/O Operations

I/O operations, such as reading from files, writing to disk, or communicating over the network, can become performance bottlenecks. By streamlining these operations, you can significantly improve throughput and reduce latency.

Use Buffered I/O

Buffered I/O minimizes the number of direct system calls, improving efficiency for both reads and writes.

Example:

```go
go
Copy
import (

    "bufio"

    "os"

)


func main() {

    file, err := os.Open("data.txt")

    if err != nil {

        panic(err)

    }

    defer file.Close()


    reader := bufio.NewReader(file)

    for {

        line, err := reader.ReadString('\n')

        if err != nil {

            break
```

```
    }

    process(line)

  }

}
```

Key Tip: Always wrap file and network I/O in buffered readers and writers when handling large amounts of data.

Minimize Latency With Concurrency

Concurrent reads or writes can help hide latency. For example, if you need to process multiple files or streams, consider processing them in parallel.

Example:

go

Copy

```
import (

  "io"

  "os"

  "sync"

)
```

```go
func copyFile(src, dest string, wg *sync.WaitGroup) {

    defer wg.Done()

    in, err := os.Open(src)

    if err != nil {

        panic(err)

    }

    defer in.Close()


    out, err := os.Create(dest)

    if err != nil {

        panic(err)

    }

    defer out.Close()


    io.Copy(out, in)

}


func main() {

    var wg sync.WaitGroup
```

```go
files := []struct{ src, dest string } {

    {"file1.txt", "file1_copy.txt"},

    {"file2.txt", "file2_copy.txt"},

    {"file3.txt", "file3_copy.txt"},

}


for _, f := range files {

    wg.Add(1)

    go copyFile(f.src, f.dest, &wg)

}


wg.Wait()

}
```

Use Efficient Data Formats

When reading or writing large datasets, choose compact data formats that reduce I/O overhead. For example:

212

- Use binary serialization instead of text formats.
- Compress data before writing to reduce size (and thus reduce I/O time).

Example:

go

Copy

```go
import (

    "bytes"

    "compress/gzip"

    "io"

)


func compressData(data []byte) []byte {

    var buf bytes.Buffer

    zw := gzip.NewWriter(&buf)

    zw.Write(data)

    zw.Close()

    return buf.Bytes()

}
```

Avoid Frequent Small Writes

Frequent small writes can be expensive. Instead, batch writes together into larger chunks to reduce the overhead.

Example:

go

Copy

```go
writer := bufio.NewWriter(file)

for _, record := range records {

    writer.WriteString(record + "\n")

}

writer.Flush()
```

Measure I/O Performance

Profile I/O-heavy code using tools like strace or Go's built-in profiling to see where time is spent. Adjust buffer sizes and concurrency levels based on the profiling results.

8.5 Handling Large Datasets and Streams

Processing large datasets or continuous streams of data requires careful memory management and efficient processing patterns to ensure stability and scalability.

214

Streaming Data Processing

Instead of reading the entire dataset into memory, process data incrementally.

Example:

go

Copy

```go
file, err := os.Open("largefile.txt")

if err != nil {

    panic(err)

}

defer file.Close()


scanner := bufio.NewScanner(file)

for scanner.Scan() {

    processLine(scanner.Text())

}

if err := scanner.Err(); err != nil {

    panic(err)

}
```

Benefits:

- Reduces memory usage.
- Allows processing to begin before the entire dataset is loaded.

Batch Processing

If streaming isn't sufficient, consider processing data in chunks or batches. This approach strikes a balance between memory usage and processing efficiency.

Example:

go

Copy

```go
const batchSize = 1000

var batch []string


file, err := os.Open("data.txt")

if err != nil {

    panic(err)

}

defer file.Close()
```

```go
scanner := bufio.NewScanner(file)

for scanner.Scan() {

    batch = append(batch, scanner.Text())

    if len(batch) >= batchSize {

        processBatch(batch)

        batch = batch[:0]

    }

}


if len(batch) > 0 {

    processBatch(batch)

}
```

Parallel and Concurrent Processing

Split large datasets into smaller pieces and process them concurrently.

Example:

go

Copy

```go
data := loadData() // Assume this returns a large dataset

chunkSize := len(data) / runtime.NumCPU()


var wg sync.WaitGroup

for i := 0; i < runtime.NumCPU(); i++ {

    start := i * chunkSize

    end := start + chunkSize

    if i == runtime.NumCPU()-1 {

        end = len(data) // Last chunk may be larger

    }


    wg.Add(1)

    go func(start, end int) {

        defer wg.Done()

        processChunk(data[start:end])

    }(start, end)

}

wg.Wait()
```

Reducing Memory Footprint

1. **Use Efficient Data Structures**
   - If possible, store large datasets in compact formats (e.g., slices of integers instead of structs with large fields).

2. **Compress Data in Memory**
   - Use compression libraries to reduce the in-memory size of large data blobs, trading some CPU time for reduced memory usage.

3. **Limit Scope of Variables**
   - Keep the scope of variables as narrow as possible. This allows the garbage collector to reclaim memory sooner.

By focusing on CPU-efficient code, optimizing I/O operations, and implementing scalable strategies for handling large datasets and streams, you can ensure that your applications maintain high performance and stability even under demanding workloads.

Chapter 9: Real-World Applications

Learning Go's fundamentals is valuable, but applying them to real-world scenarios is what truly brings your skills to life. This chapter focuses on two common use cases: building a REST API and creating command-line tools and utilities.

9.1 Building a REST API Using Go

REST APIs are the backbone of many modern applications, and Go's net/http package provides all the necessary tools to build simple, robust, and efficient APIs without needing additional frameworks.

Setting Up a Simple REST API

1. Project Structure A typical Go REST API project might look like:

go

Copy

```
rest-api/
├── main.go
├── handlers/
│   ├── user.go
├── models/
│   ├── user.go
```

```
└── go.mod
```

---

2. Handling HTTP Requests

The net/http package enables routing and handling HTTP requests. You define a handler function that processes requests and writes responses.

Example:

go

Copy

```go
package main

import (
    "encoding/json"
    "net/http"
)

type User struct {
    ID   int    `json:"id"`
    Name string `json:"name"`
```

```go
}


func getUserHandler(w http.ResponseWriter, r *http.Request) {

    user := User{ID: 1, Name: "John Doe"}

    w.Header().Set("Content-Type", "application/json")

    json.NewEncoder(w).Encode(user)

}


func main() {

    http.HandleFunc("/user", getUserHandler)

    http.ListenAndServe(":8080", nil)

}
```

How It Works:

- http.HandleFunc associates the /user endpoint with the getUserHandler function.
- json.NewEncoder(w).Encode(user) serializes the user struct to JSON and sends it as a response.
- http.ListenAndServe(":8080", nil) starts the server on port 8080.

---

3. Adding Routes and Methods

You can extend your API by adding more routes and handling different HTTP methods.

Example:

go

Copy

```go
package main

import (
    "encoding/json"
    "net/http"
    "strconv"
)

type User struct {
    ID   int    `json:"id"`
    Name string `json:"name"`
}

var users = []User{
```

```go
    {ID: 1, Name: "John Doe"},

    {ID: 2, Name: "Jane Smith"},

}


func getUsersHandler(w http.ResponseWriter, r *http.Request) {

    w.Header().Set("Content-Type", "application/json")

    json.NewEncoder(w).Encode(users)

}


func getUserHandler(w http.ResponseWriter, r *http.Request) {

    idParam := r.URL.Query().Get("id")

    id, err := strconv.Atoi(idParam)

    if err != nil {

        http.Error(w, "Invalid ID", http.StatusBadRequest)

        return

    }


    for _, user := range users {

        if user.ID == id {
```

```go
        w.Header().Set("Content-Type", "application/json")

        json.NewEncoder(w).Encode(user)

        return

    }

}


    http.NotFound(w, r)

}


func main() {

    http.HandleFunc("/users", getUsersHandler)

    http.HandleFunc("/user", getUserHandler)

    http.ListenAndServe(":8080", nil)

}
```

Adding Middleware

Middleware functions can handle cross-cutting concerns, such as logging, authentication, or CORS.

Example:

go

Copy

```go
func loggingMiddleware(next http.Handler) http.Handler {
    return http.HandlerFunc(func(w http.ResponseWriter, r *http.Request) {
        log.Printf("%s %s\n", r.Method, r.URL.Path)
        next.ServeHTTP(w, r)
    })
}


func main() {
    mux := http.NewServeMux()
    mux.HandleFunc("/users", getUsersHandler)
    mux.HandleFunc("/user", getUserHandler)


    wrappedMux := loggingMiddleware(mux)
    http.ListenAndServe(":8080", wrappedMux)
}
```

Key Tips for Building REST APIs

1. **Use net/http for simplicity:** You can start small without introducing third-party frameworks.
2. **Handle errors gracefully:** Return proper HTTP status codes and informative messages.
3. **Follow REST conventions:** Use proper HTTP methods (GET, POST, PUT, DELETE) and meaningful endpoints.
4. **Keep it modular:** Organize your handlers, models, and middleware into separate packages for maintainability.

9.2 Creating Command-Line Tools and Utilities

Command-line tools are another area where Go excels. The language's portability, ease of compilation, and performance make it a great choice for creating standalone utilities that run on any platform.

Simple Command-Line Application

Example: A Hello World CLI

go

Copy

```
package main
```

```go
import (

    "flag"

    "fmt"

)


func main() {

    name := flag.String("name", "World", "a name to say hello to")

    flag.Parse()

    fmt.Printf("Hello, %s!\n", *name)

}
```

How It Works:

- flag.String defines a command-line flag. The -name flag can be set by running the program with -name=John.
- flag.Parse parses the flags provided at runtime.
- The *name dereferences the flag's pointer to get the value.

Adding Subcommands

More complex tools often have subcommands (like git commit or kubectl apply).

Example:

go

Copy

```go
package main

import (
    "flag"
    "fmt"
    "os"
)

func main() {
    // Define subcommands
    helloCmd := flag.NewFlagSet("hello", flag.ExitOnError)
    name := helloCmd.String("name", "World", "a name to say hello to")

    sumCmd := flag.NewFlagSet("sum", flag.ExitOnError)
    num1 := sumCmd.Int("a", 0, "first number")
    num2 := sumCmd.Int("b", 0, "second number")
```

```go
// Parse subcommands

if len(os.Args) < 2 {

    fmt.Println("expected 'hello' or 'sum' subcommands")

    os.Exit(1)

}


switch os.Args[1] {

case "hello":

    helloCmd.Parse(os.Args[2:])

    fmt.Printf("Hello, %s!\n", *name)

case "sum":

    sumCmd.Parse(os.Args[2:])

    fmt.Printf("Sum: %d\n", *num1+*num2)

default:

    fmt.Println("unknown command")

    os.Exit(1)

}

}
```

Usage:

sh

Copy

```
./tool hello -name=John

./tool sum -a=10 -b=20
```

Reading Environment Variables

Command-line tools often rely on environment variables for configuration.

Example:

go

Copy

```go
package main


import (

    "fmt"

    "os"

)
```

```go
func main() {

    dbURL := os.Getenv("DB_URL")

    if dbURL == "" {

        fmt.Println("DB_URL is not set")

        os.Exit(1)

    }


    fmt.Printf("Connecting to database at %s\n", dbURL)

}
```

Key Tip: Combine environment variables, flags, and configuration files for maximum flexibility.

Working With Files and I/O

Command-line tools frequently process files or directories.

Example:

go

Copy

```go
package main

import (

	"bufio"

	"fmt"

	"os"

)

func main() {

	file, err := os.Open("input.txt")

	if err != nil {

		fmt.Println("Error:", err)

		os.Exit(1)

	}

	defer file.Close()


	scanner := bufio.NewScanner(file)

	for scanner.Scan() {

		fmt.Println(scanner.Text())
```

```
    }

    if err := scanner.Err(); err != nil {

        fmt.Println("Error:", err)

    }

}
```

Key Tips for Command-Line Tools

1. **Handle errors gracefully:** Provide clear messages and use appropriate exit codes.
2. **Follow UNIX conventions:** Make the tool composable, with meaningful flags and environment variables.
3. **Cross-platform support:** Ensure the code works seamlessly on multiple operating systems.
4. **Keep the tool small and focused:** Each command or subcommand should do one thing well.

By building REST APIs and command-line tools, you not only strengthen your Go skills but also develop highly practical applications that can serve as the foundation for real-world projects.

9.3 Developing Microservices With gRPC and HTTP/2

gRPC is a modern, high-performance RPC framework that uses **Protocol Buffers** (Protobuf) for serialization. It's ideal for microservices that need efficient communication over HTTP/2 and supports multiple languages, making it a great choice for distributed systems.

Why gRPC for Microservices?

1. **Efficient Serialization:**
   Protobuf is more compact than JSON, resulting in lower bandwidth usage and faster serialization/deserialization.

2. **Built-In Code Generation:**
   Protobuf generates client and server code, ensuring type safety and reducing boilerplate.

3. **Streaming Support:**
   gRPC's bidirectional streaming allows for efficient real-time communication between services.

4. **HTTP/2 Features:**
   gRPC takes full advantage of HTTP/2, including multiplexing, flow control, and low-latency connections.

Getting Started With gRPC in Go

1. Define Your Protobuf Service Create a .proto file that describes your service's API:

proto

Copy

235

```proto
syntax = "proto3";

package example;

service Greeter {
  rpc SayHello (HelloRequest) returns (HelloResponse);
}

message HelloRequest {
  string name = 1;
}

message HelloResponse {
  string message = 1;
}
```

2. Generate Go Code Use the protoc compiler with the Go plugin:

sh

Copy

```
protoc --go_out=. --go-grpc_out=. example.proto
```

This generates a .pb.go file and a _grpc.pb.go file.

3. Implement the Server

go

Copy

```go
package main

import (
    "context"
    "log"
    "net"

    pb "example/proto" // Replace with your generated package
    "google.golang.org/grpc"
)

type server struct {
    pb.UnimplementedGreeterServer
```

```go
}


func (s *server) SayHello(ctx context.Context, req *pb.HelloRequest)
(*pb.HelloResponse, error) {
    return &pb.HelloResponse{Message: "Hello, " + req.GetName()}, nil
}


func main() {
    lis, err := net.Listen("tcp", ":50051")
    if err != nil {
        log.Fatalf("failed to listen: %v", err)
    }
    grpcServer := grpc.NewServer()
    pb.RegisterGreeterServer(grpcServer, &server{})


    log.Println("Server listening on port 50051")
    if err := grpcServer.Serve(lis); err != nil {
        log.Fatalf("failed to serve: %v", err)
    }
}
```

}

4. Write a Client

go

Copy

```go
package main

import (
    "context"
    "log"
    "time"

    pb "example/proto" // Replace with your generated package
    "google.golang.org/grpc"
)

func main() {
    conn, err := grpc.Dial("localhost:50051", grpc.WithInsecure())
    if err != nil {
```

```go
        log.Fatalf("did not connect: %v", err)
    }

    defer conn.Close()

    client := pb.NewGreeterClient(conn)
    ctx, cancel := context.WithTimeout(context.Background(), time.Second)
    defer cancel()

    resp, err := client.SayHello(ctx, &pb.HelloRequest{Name: "World"})
    if err != nil {
        log.Fatalf("could not greet: %v", err)
    }
    log.Printf("Greeting: %s", resp.GetMessage())
}
```

Advanced gRPC Features

1. **Streaming RPCs:**
   gRPC supports **unary, server-streaming, client-streaming**, and

bidirectional-streaming calls, making it ideal for real-time updates and large datasets.

2. **Interceptors for Middleware:**
   Use interceptors for logging, authentication, rate limiting, and metrics.

3. **gRPC Gateway:**
   Expose a RESTful JSON API alongside your gRPC service by using gRPC Gateway. This enables clients that don't support gRPC to communicate via traditional HTTP/1.1 endpoints.

---

gRPC and HTTP/2 Benefits in Microservices

1. **Multiplexed Streams:**
   Send multiple gRPC calls over a single connection, improving efficiency and reducing latency.

2. **Flow Control:**
   HTTP/2 flow control helps ensure stable performance under load.

3. **Improved Security:**
   gRPC's strong integration with TLS and mTLS provides robust security out of the box.

9.4 Using Go for Serverless Applications

Serverless computing platforms—like AWS Lambda, Google Cloud Functions, and Azure Functions—allow developers to focus on writing code without worrying about managing servers. Go's fast startup times and low resource usage make it an excellent choice for serverless workloads.

Why Use Go for Serverless?

1. **Low Overhead:**

   Go binaries are lightweight and have quick cold-start times.

2. **Native Concurrency:**

   Goroutines make it easier to handle parallel tasks within a single function.

3. **Strong Ecosystem:**

   With well-maintained libraries and clear tooling, Go simplifies integrating with serverless platforms.

AWS Lambda Example

1. Write Your Function:

go

Copy

```go
package main

import (

    "context"

    "github.com/aws/aws-lambda-go/lambda"

)


type MyEvent struct {
```

```go
    Name string `json:"name"`

}


type MyResponse struct {

    Message string `json:"message"`

}


func handler(ctx context.Context, event MyEvent) (MyResponse, error) {

    return MyResponse{Message: "Hello, " + event.Name}, nil

}


func main() {

    lambda.Start(handler)

}
```

2. Build and Deploy:

Build your Go code:
sh
Copy
```sh
GOOS=linux GOARCH=amd64 go build -o main main.go
```

Package it:

sh

Copy

zip function.zip main

- Deploy to AWS Lambda using the AWS CLI or a serverless framework.

Google Cloud Functions Example

1. Write Your Function:

go

Copy

```
package hello


import (

    "fmt"

    "net/http"

)


func HelloWorld(w http.ResponseWriter, r *http.Request) {

    fmt.Fprint(w, "Hello, World!")

}
```

244

2. Deploy Using gcloud:

sh

Copy

```
gcloud functions deploy HelloWorld \
  --runtime go116 \
  --trigger-http \
  --allow-unauthenticated
```

Best Practices for Go Serverless

1. **Minimize Cold-Start Time:**
   Reduce binary size and package dependencies to shorten initialization times.

2. **Use Context Effectively:**
   Rely on the context.Context provided by serverless platforms to handle deadlines, cancellations, and request metadata.

3. **Keep Functions Small and Focused:**
   A single function should handle one logical operation. This simplifies testing, deployment, and maintenance.

9.5 Integrating Go With Cloud Platforms (AWS, GCP, Azure)

Go's rich set of libraries and tools make it a natural fit for cloud-native development. Integrating with major cloud providers enables you to build scalable, secure, and resilient applications.

AWS SDK for Go

Install the AWS SDK:
sh

Copy

go get github.com/aws/aws-sdk-go-v2

1. **Example: Listing S3 Buckets**

   go

   Copy

   package main

import (

   "context"

   "fmt"

   "log"

   "github.com/aws/aws-sdk-go-v2/config"

   "github.com/aws/aws-sdk-go-v2/service/s3"

246

```go
)


func main() {

    cfg, err := config.LoadDefaultConfig(context.TODO())

    if err != nil {

        log.Fatalf("unable to load SDK config, %v", err)

    }


    client := s3.NewFromConfig(cfg)


    result, err := client.ListBuckets(context.TODO(), &s3.ListBucketsInput{})

    if err != nil {

        log.Fatalf("unable to list buckets, %v", err)

    }


    for _, bucket := range result.Buckets {

        fmt.Println("Bucket:", *bucket.Name)

    }

}
```

Google Cloud Go Libraries

Install the GCP SDK:

sh

Copy

go get cloud.google.com/go/storage

1. **Example: Uploading a File to GCS**

   go

   Copy

   package main

```go
import (

    "context"

    "fmt"

    "os"


    "cloud.google.com/go/storage"

)


func main() {

    ctx := context.Background()
```

```go
client, err := storage.NewClient(ctx)

if err != nil {

    fmt.Println("Error creating client:", err)

    return

}

defer client.Close()


bucket := "my-gcs-bucket"

object := "example.txt"

data := []byte("Hello, Cloud Storage!")


wc := client.Bucket(bucket).Object(object).NewWriter(ctx)

if _, err := wc.Write(data); err != nil {

    fmt.Println("Error writing to object:", err)

}

if err := wc.Close(); err != nil {

    fmt.Println("Error closing object writer:", err)

}
```

```go
fmt.Printf("Uploaded %s to %s\n", object, bucket)
}
```

Azure SDK for Go

Install the Azure SDK:

sh

Copy

go get github.com/Azure/azure-sdk-for-go/sdk/storage/azblob

1. **Example: Uploading a Blob to Azure Storage**

   go

   Copy

   package main

import (

  "context"

  "fmt"

  "os"

  "github.com/Azure/azure-sdk-for-go/sdk/storage/azblob"

)

```go
func main() {

    accountName := os.Getenv("AZURE_STORAGE_ACCOUNT")

    accountKey := os.Getenv("AZURE_STORAGE_KEY")

    containerName := "mycontainer"

    blobName := "example.txt"

    blobData := []byte("Hello, Azure Blob Storage!")


    credential, err := azblob.NewSharedKeyCredential(accountName, accountKey)
    if err != nil {

        fmt.Println("Error creating credential:", err)

        return

    }


    serviceClient, err :=
azblob.NewServiceClient(fmt.Sprintf("https://%s.blob.core.windows.net/",
accountName), credential, nil)

    if err != nil {

        fmt.Println("Error creating service client:", err)

        return

    }
```

```go
containerClient := serviceClient.NewContainerClient(containerName)

blobClient := containerClient.NewBlobClient(blobName)


_, err = blobClient.UploadBuffer(context.Background(), blobData, nil)

if err != nil {

    fmt.Println("Error uploading blob:", err)

}


fmt.Printf("Uploaded blob %s to container %s\n", blobName, containerName)

}
```

Best Practices for Cloud Integrations

1. **Use Environment Variables for Credentials:**
   Avoid hardcoding sensitive credentials. Instead, use environment variables or secrets managers.

2. **Enable Observability:**
   Integrate cloud monitoring tools to track metrics, logs, and traces.

3. **Leverage Cloud SDK Documentation:**
   Each provider's Go SDK documentation offers detailed examples and best practices for using their APIs.

By utilizing gRPC for efficient microservice communication, adopting serverless paradigms, and seamlessly integrating with major cloud platforms, you can build scalable, reliable, and maintainable cloud-native applications in Go

Chapter 10: Go in Production

Once you've developed a Go application, the next challenge is deploying it to production. This chapter focuses on best practices for deploying Go applications and how to containerize them using Docker.

10.1 Deployment Best Practices for Go Applications

Deploying a Go application to production involves more than just shipping a binary. Following best practices ensures smooth, reliable, and maintainable deployments.

---

1. Build Static Binaries

One of Go's greatest advantages is the ability to produce self-contained static binaries. By using the CGO_ENABLED=0 environment variable, you can ensure your binary has no external dependencies, making it portable and easy to run on different environments.

Example:

```sh
Copy
CGO_ENABLED=0 GOOS=linux GOARCH=amd64 go build -o myapp main.go
```

---

2. Use Environment Variables for Configuration

Avoid hardcoding environment-specific values. Instead, use environment variables to manage configuration details such as database connection strings, API keys, or service endpoints. This approach simplifies moving from development to staging to production environments without code changes.

Example:

go
Copy

```go
package main

import (
    "fmt"
    "os"
)

func main() {
    dbHost := os.Getenv("DB_HOST")
    if dbHost == "" {
        dbHost = "localhost"
    }
    fmt.Println("Connecting to DB at:", dbHost)
}
```

---

3. Leverage a Process Manager or Supervisor

In production, a process manager or service supervisor can ensure that your application restarts if it crashes and handles log rotation or resource limits. Common choices include:

- **Systemd**: Manages services on many Linux distributions.
- **Supervisor**: A lightweight and flexible process control system.

255

4. Logging and Metrics

- **Structured Logging:** Use a structured logging library (like logrus or zap) to produce logs that are easy to parse and monitor.
- **Export Metrics:** Integrate with Prometheus or another monitoring system to expose metrics via an HTTP endpoint. This enables you to track application health, performance, and usage patterns.

Example of a metrics endpoint:

```go
Copy
package main

import (
    "net/http"

    "github.com/prometheus/client_golang/prometheus"
    "github.com/prometheus/client_golang/prometheus/promhttp"
)

var (
    requestCount = prometheus.NewCounter(prometheus.CounterOpts{
        Name: "http_requests_total",
        Help: "Total number of HTTP requests",
    })
)

func main() {
    prometheus.MustRegister(requestCount)
```

```go
    http.Handle("/metrics", promhttp.Handler())
    http.HandleFunc("/", func(w http.ResponseWriter, r *http.Request) {
        requestCount.Inc()
        w.Write([]byte("Hello, world!"))
    })

    http.ListenAndServe(":8080", nil)
}
```

---

5. Graceful Shutdown

Ensure that your application shuts down gracefully by handling termination signals (e.g., SIGTERM). This allows you to close connections, flush logs, and clean up resources before exiting.

Example:

go
Copy
```go
package main

import (
    "context"
    "log"
    "net/http"
    "os"
    "os/signal"
    "time"
)
```

257

```go
func main() {
    server := &http.Server{Addr: ":8080"}

    go func() {
        if err := server.ListenAndServe(); err != nil && err != http.ErrServerClosed {
            log.Fatalf("Server failed: %v", err)
        }
    }()

    stop := make(chan os.Signal, 1)
    signal.Notify(stop, os.Interrupt)
    <-stop

    log.Println("Shutting down gracefully...")
    ctx, cancel := context.WithTimeout(context.Background(), 5*time.Second)
    defer cancel()

    if err := server.Shutdown(ctx); err != nil {
        log.Fatalf("Server shutdown failed: %v", err)
    }
    log.Println("Server exited")
}
```

---

6. Security Best Practices

- **Use HTTPS:** Secure all communications. Use certificates from a trusted provider or an automated service like Let's Encrypt.
- **Limit Permissions:** Run your application as a non-root user whenever possible.

- **Keep Dependencies Updated:** Regularly update libraries and runtime dependencies to address security vulnerabilities.

---

7. Documentation and Runbooks

Maintain clear documentation on how to start, stop, and debug the application. Include details on environment variables, logging formats, metrics endpoints, and troubleshooting steps.

10.2 Dockerizing Your Go Applications

Containerization simplifies deployments, ensures consistency across environments, and isolates dependencies. Docker is the industry standard for packaging applications and their dependencies into portable containers.

Step 1: Create a Simple Dockerfile

A basic Dockerfile for a Go application might look like this:

dockerfile
Copy

```
# Stage 1: Build the binary
FROM golang:1.20 as builder

WORKDIR /app

# Cache dependencies before building
COPY go.mod go.sum ./
```

```
RUN go mod download

# Build the application
COPY . .
RUN CGO_ENABLED=0 GOOS=linux go build -o main .

# Stage 2: Create the minimal image
FROM alpine:3.16

# Add CA certificates
RUN apk --no-cache add ca-certificates

WORKDIR /root/

# Copy the binary from the builder stage
COPY --from=builder /app/main .

# Run the binary
ENTRYPOINT ["./main"]
```

Step 2: Build and Run the Docker Image

Build the image:

sh

Copy

```
docker build -t myapp:latest .
```

1. Run the container:

sh

Copy

```
docker run -d -p 8080:8080 --name myapp myapp:latest
```

2. Test the application:

sh

Copy

```
curl http://localhost:8080
```

Step 3: Optimize the Dockerfile

1. **Multi-Stage Builds:**

   The example above uses multi-stage builds, which reduce the final image size by separating the build environment from the runtime environment.

2. **Use a Minimal Base Image:**

   Using alpine or distroless images reduces the attack surface and keeps the image small.

Exclude Unnecessary Files:

Use a .dockerignore file to prevent copying unnecessary files into the image:

bash

Copy

```
.git
*.log
tmp/
```

Step 4: Environment Variables and Config Files

Pass environment variables to the container:

sh

Copy

docker run -d -p 8080:8080 -e DB_HOST=prod-db.example.com myapp:latest

Or use a configuration file mounted at runtime:

sh

Copy

docker run -d -p 8080:8080 -v $(pwd)/config:/app/config myapp:latest

---

Step 5: Docker Compose for Multi-Container Setups

If your Go application depends on other services (like databases, caches, or queues), Docker Compose simplifies the setup.

Example docker-compose.yml:

yaml

Copy

```
version: "3.8"
services:
  app:
    build:
      context: .
      dockerfile: Dockerfile
    ports:
      - "8080:8080"
    environment:
      - DB_HOST=db
```

262

```
db:
  image: postgres:14
  environment:
    POSTGRES_USER: user
    POSTGRES_PASSWORD: password
    POSTGRES_DB=example
```

Start everything with:

sh

Copy

```
docker-compose up
```

Best Practices for Dockerizing Go Applications

1. **Keep Images Small:**
   - Use multi-stage builds.
   - Only include what's necessary for production.
2. **Use Tagged Versions:**
   - Pin dependencies and base images to specific versions to ensure reproducibility.
3. **Scan Images for Vulnerabilities:**
   - Use tools like docker scan or trivy to detect and address known vulnerabilities.
4. **Leverage Build Caches:**
   - Arrange Dockerfile instructions to take advantage of layer caching, reducing build times.

By following deployment best practices and containerizing your Go applications with Docker, you can streamline production setups, ensure consistency, and enhance the overall reliability of your services.

10.3 Monitoring and Logging With Go

Monitoring and logging are critical for maintaining application reliability in production. They provide insight into application health, performance, and unexpected issues, allowing you to respond quickly and maintain smooth operations.

Structured Logging

Why Use Structured Logs?

Structured logs—key-value pairs rather than plain text messages—make it easier to filter, search, and analyze log data.

Example:

go
Copy
```go
package main

import (
    "log"

    "go.uber.org/zap"
)

func main() {
    logger, err := zap.NewProduction()
    if err != nil {
```

```go
    log.Fatalf("can't initialize zap logger: %v", err)
}
defer logger.Sync()

logger.Info("Application started",
    zap.String("version", "1.0.0"),
    zap.Int("port", 8080),
)
}
```

Benefits:

- **Better Filtering:** Quickly find all logs related to a specific request or user.
- **Integrations:** Feed structured logs into logging systems like ELK (Elasticsearch, Logstash, Kibana) or Loki+Grafana.

Exporting Metrics

Why Metrics Matter:
Metrics provide real-time insight into application performance, resource usage, and throughput.

Example: Exposing Prometheus Metrics

go
Copy
```go
package main

import (
    "net/http"
```

```go
    "github.com/prometheus/client_golang/prometheus"
    "github.com/prometheus/client_golang/prometheus/promhttp"
)

var (
    requestCount = prometheus.NewCounter(prometheus.CounterOpts{
        Name: "http_requests_total",
        Help: "Total number of HTTP requests",
    })
)

func main() {
    prometheus.MustRegister(requestCount)

    http.Handle("/metrics", promhttp.Handler())
    http.HandleFunc("/", func(w http.ResponseWriter, r *http.Request) {
        requestCount.Inc()
        w.Write([]byte("Hello, world!"))
    })

    http.ListenAndServe(":8080", nil)
}
```

Tools:

- **Prometheus:** Pulls metrics and offers alerting.
- **Grafana:** Visualizes metrics, providing dashboards for application performance and health.

Distributed Tracing

Distributed tracing helps pinpoint performance bottlenecks and track requests across microservices. Tools like OpenTelemetry, Jaeger, or Zipkin integrate well with Go.

Example: Integrating OpenTelemetry

1. **Set up an OpenTelemetry tracer.**
2. **Instrument your code to start spans around critical operations.**
3. **Export traces to a backend (Jaeger, Zipkin, etc.).**

Key Tracing Concepts:

- **Spans:** Represent individual operations within a request.
- **Context Propagation:** Allows tracing information to follow a request across service boundaries.

Log Aggregation and Centralization

In production, logs are often stored centrally for easy access and analysis:

- **Centralized Logging Tools:**
  - **Fluentd/Logstash:** Aggregate logs from multiple instances.
  - **Elastic Stack (ELK):** Search and analyze logs efficiently.
  - **Loki:** Lightweight logging for Kubernetes.
- **Cloud Logging Services:**
  - **AWS CloudWatch, Google Cloud Logging, Azure Monitor:** Managed solutions that simplify log collection, storage, and analysis.

Best Practices:

- **Add Request Identifiers:** Include unique request IDs in logs to track issues end-to-end.
- **Capture Contextual Data:** Log the relevant environment, user, and event details.

Alerting and Dashboards

Set up alerts based on metrics and logs to detect issues early:

- **Threshold Alerts:** Trigger when response time or error rates exceed acceptable levels.
- **Anomaly Detection:** Identify patterns that deviate from normal behavior.
- **Visual Dashboards:** Use Grafana or another tool to create intuitive, real-time dashboards.

10.4 Using Kubernetes for Scalability

Kubernetes is an industry-standard orchestration platform that simplifies deploying, scaling, and managing containerized applications.

Why Kubernetes for Go Applications?

1. **Automated Scaling:**
   Kubernetes scales workloads up or down based on CPU/memory usage or custom metrics.

2. **Self-Healing:**

   If a container crashes, Kubernetes automatically restarts it. Failed nodes are rescheduled on healthy nodes.

3. **Service Discovery and Load Balancing:**

   Built-in service discovery and load balancing simplify communication between services.

Deploying a Go Application on Kubernetes

1. Create a Docker Image:

Ensure your application is containerized.

Example:

sh

Copy

```
docker build -t myapp:v1 .
```

2. Write a Kubernetes Deployment Manifest:

yaml

Copy

```
# deployment.yaml
apiVersion: apps/v1
kind: Deployment
metadata:
  name: myapp
spec:
  replicas: 3
  selector:
```

```yaml
    matchLabels:
      app: myapp
  template:
    metadata:
      labels:
        app: myapp
    spec:
      containers:
      - name: myapp
        image: myapp:v1
        ports:
        - containerPort: 8080
```

3. Write a Service Manifest for Networking:

yaml

Copy

```yaml
# service.yaml
apiVersion: v1
kind: Service
metadata:
  name: myapp-service
spec:
  selector:
    app: myapp
  ports:
  - protocol: TCP
    port: 80
    targetPort: 8080
  type: LoadBalancer
```

270

4. Apply the Manifests:

sh

Copy

```
kubectl apply -f deployment.yaml
kubectl apply -f service.yaml
```

Scaling and Updates

Horizontal Pod Autoscaling:
Add an autoscaler that increases replicas when CPU usage spikes.

sh

Copy

```
kubectl autoscale deployment myapp --cpu-percent=50 --min=2 --max=10
```

Rolling Updates:
Update your application version without downtime.

sh

Copy

```
kubectl set image deployment/myapp myapp=myapp:v2
```

Key Benefits:

- Seamless scaling based on demand.
- Built-in resilience through health checks and rolling updates.
- Simplified management of complex, distributed systems.

Monitoring Kubernetes Clusters

Integrate Kubernetes metrics and logs into your monitoring stack:

- **Kube-state-metrics:** Provides Kubernetes cluster metrics.
- **Prometheus Operator:** Simplifies Prometheus deployment and integration.
- **Grafana Dashboards:** Visualize pod performance, resource usage, and health.

10.5 CI/CD Pipelines for Go Projects

Continuous Integration (CI) and Continuous Deployment/Delivery (CD) automate the process of building, testing, and deploying Go applications. A well-designed CI/CD pipeline reduces manual effort, ensures consistent quality, and speeds up delivery.

Setting Up a CI/CD Pipeline

1. Continuous Integration (CI):

- **Run Tests:**
  Automate unit tests, integration tests, and linting after every code push.
- **Static Analysis:**
  Use tools like golangci-lint to enforce coding standards.

Example Workflow:

- Developer pushes code to a Git branch.
- CI pipeline triggers automatically.
- Steps:
    - Fetch dependencies (go mod tidy).

- o Run static analysis (golangci-lint run).
- o Run tests (go test ./...).
- On success, the pipeline may tag a release or build a Docker image.

2. Continuous Deployment/Delivery (CD):

- **Deploy to Staging:**
  If all CI steps pass, automatically deploy to a staging environment.
- **Approval Gates:**
  Require manual approval before deploying to production, or automate it if confidence is high.
- **Production Deployment:**
  Push the Docker image to a container registry (like Docker Hub, ECR, GCR) and deploy it using Kubernetes manifests or Helm charts.

Popular CI/CD Tools

1. **GitHub Actions:**
   - o Native integration with GitHub repositories.
   - o Define workflows in .github/workflows using YAML.
   - o Supports testing, building, and deploying Go applications.
2. **GitLab CI/CD:**
   - o Built into GitLab.
   - o Define pipelines in .gitlab-ci.yml.
   - o Offers robust integration with Kubernetes.
3. **CircleCI:**
   - o Hosted CI/CD with simple configuration.
   - o Integrates well with Docker workflows.
4. **Jenkins:**
   - o Highly customizable and extensible.

- ○ Works well for complex enterprise pipelines.

Example: GitHub Actions Workflow

.github/workflows/ci.yml:

yaml
Copy

```
name: CI

on:
  push:
    branches:
      - main

jobs:
  build:
    runs-on: ubuntu-latest

    steps:
      - name: Checkout code
        uses: actions/checkout@v3

      - name: Set up Go
        uses: actions/setup-go@v4
        with:
          go-version: 1.20

      - name: Install dependencies
        run: go mod tidy
```

```
- name: Run tests
  run: go test ./...

- name: Build Docker image
  run: |
    docker build -t myapp:v1 .
```

Best Practices for CI/CD Pipelines

1. **Fail Fast:**
   Quickly detect and report failures to minimize wasted time.

2. **Run Tests in Parallel:**
   Parallelize unit tests, integration tests, and linting for faster feedback.

3. **Use Secrets Management:**
   Safely store and use API keys, credentials, and sensitive information.

4. **Incremental Builds:**
   Cache dependencies and intermediate build steps to reduce build times.

5. **Embrace Infrastructure-as-Code:**
   Automate the deployment of pipelines and infrastructure using tools like Terraform or Helm.

By integrating structured logging, comprehensive monitoring, Kubernetes-based scaling, and CI/CD pipelines, you can take your Go applications from development to production in a streamlined, scalable, and reliable manner.

Chapter 11: Community, Tools, and Resources

The Go ecosystem is supported by a vibrant open-source community and a robust set of tools. Together, these resources help developers write better code, adhere to standards, debug effectively, and stay up to date with the latest best practices.

11.1 Go's Open-Source Community: Libraries and Frameworks

Go's simplicity and efficiency have inspired a broad community of developers who create open-source libraries and frameworks that cover a wide range of use cases.

Popular Go Libraries

1. **Web Frameworks:**
   - **Gin:** A fast, minimalist HTTP web framework that simplifies building REST APIs.
   - **Echo:** Another high-performance web framework that includes built-in middleware and support for JSON and XML rendering.

2. **Database Interaction:**
   - **GORM:** A full-featured ORM that simplifies database operations, migrations, and model relationships.
   - **sqlx:** Extends Go's database/sql package with useful abstractions like named queries and automatic struct mapping.

3. **Authentication and Security:**
   - **oauth2:** The official Go library for implementing OAuth 2.0 clients and servers.
   - **gorilla/securecookie:** Handles secure, cookie-based sessions with built-in encryption.

4. **Concurrency and Messaging:**
   - **goroutines:** Not a library, but leveraging native goroutines and channels is a cornerstone of Go's concurrency model.
   - **nsq:** A real-time distributed messaging platform written in Go, often used for pub-sub patterns.
5. **Testing and Mocking:**
   - **testify:** Provides easy-to-use assertions and mocking capabilities for unit tests.
   - **gomock:** A powerful mocking library that works seamlessly with Go's interfaces.

Community Platforms and Events

1. **Go User Groups and Meetups:**
   - Local Go user groups exist in many cities worldwide, providing networking and learning opportunities.
2. **Online Forums:**
   - **Go Forum (forum.golangbridge.org):** A place to ask questions, share knowledge, and discuss Go-related topics.
3. **Conferences:**
   - **GopherCon:** The premier Go conference, held annually, offering keynotes, technical sessions, and workshops.

Open-Source Collaboration

The open-source Go community is highly active on GitHub. Key project repositories include:

- **golang/go:** The official Go language repository where you can report issues, propose changes, and contribute.
- **golang/tools:** A repository of official Go tools, including gopls (the Go language server).

Staying Updated

- **Go Blog (blog.golang.org):** Regular posts from the Go team covering new features, releases, and best practices.
- **Go Weekly:** A curated newsletter highlighting community projects, blog posts, and upcoming events.
- **Gopher Slack (invite at gophers.slack.com):** A community chat for discussing all things Go, with channels for various topics.

11.2 Essential Tools for Go Developers

The Go toolchain includes several built-in commands (like go test and go build) that streamline the development process. Beyond these basics, a number of additional tools are widely used in the community.

---

gofmt

Purpose:
Ensures that Go code is formatted consistently according to the language's conventions.

Usage:

sh

Copy

```
gofmt -w yourfile.go
```

Benefits:

- Enforces a single, standard code style across projects.
- Eliminates debates over code formatting.
- Simplifies code reviews by ensuring formatting is not an issue.

Example: Before:

go

Copy

```
func main() {
    fmt.Println("Hello, world!")
    fmt.Println("Go is awesome")
    }
```

After running gofmt:

go

Copy

```
func main() {
    fmt.Println("Hello, world!")
    fmt.Println("Go is awesome")
}
```

---

golangci-lint

Purpose:

Aggregates multiple linters into one tool, helping identify code issues early.

Features:

- Runs static analysis checks.
- Detects common problems, including unused variables, error handling issues, and performance inefficiencies.
- Configurable rules to suit project needs.

Installation:

sh

Copy

```
go install github.com/golangci/golangci-lint/cmd/golangci-lint@latest
```

Usage:

sh

Copy

```
golangci-lint run
```

Common Checks:

- **Unused variables/functions.**
- **Inefficient loop structures.**
- **Error handling improvements.**

By integrating golangci-lint into your CI pipeline, you can catch bugs and inconsistencies before they make it into production.

---

delve

Purpose:

A full-featured debugger designed specifically for Go.

Features:

- Step through code line-by-line.
- Inspect variable values at runtime.
- Set breakpoints and conditional breakpoints.
- Examine call stacks and goroutine states.

Installation:

sh

Copy

go install github.com/go-delve/delve/cmd/dlv@latest

Common Commands:

Start debugging:

sh

Copy

dlv debug main.go

Set a breakpoint:

sh

Copy

(dlv) break main.go:10

Run the program:

sh

Copy

(dlv) continue

281

- **Inspect a variable:**

  sh

  Copy

  (dlv) print myVar

- **Integration With IDEs:**

- **VS Code:** Use the Go extension to seamlessly debug with Delve.
- **GoLand:** Includes built-in Delve integration.

Benefits:

- Makes it easy to diagnose and fix complex issues.
- Provides detailed insights into runtime behavior.
- Especially useful for debugging concurrency problems.

Bringing It All Together

By leveraging gofmt, golangci-lint, and delve, you ensure that your code is:

1. **Consistently formatted:** Everyone on the team follows the same style.
2. **Thoroughly analyzed:** Issues are caught early, before they lead to bugs.
3. **Effectively debugged:** Problems are identified and resolved faster.

Combined with Go's open-source community, libraries, and frameworks, these tools help developers produce high-quality code more efficiently

11.3 Staying Updated With Go Releases

The Go programming language is constantly evolving, with new features, performance improvements, and bug fixes introduced in each release. Staying informed about these updates helps developers take full advantage of the language's capabilities and keep their codebase up-to-date.

Official Go Release Cycle

Go follows a predictable, twice-yearly release cycle:

- **Major releases:** Typically occur every February and August.
- **Security and bug fixes:** Released as needed between major versions.

Where to Find Release Notes:

- **Go Blog (blog.golang.org):** Each release is accompanied by detailed posts explaining new features, changes, and deprecations.
- **Official Release Notes (golang.org/doc/devel/release.html):** A concise, authoritative summary of what's new and improved.

Tools for Staying Updated

1. **Go Toolchain Management Tools:**
   - go install golang.org/dl/go1.X@latest: Install a specific version of Go locally to test new features before fully upgrading.
   - **Third-party managers like gvm or asdf:** Make it easy to switch between multiple Go versions.
2. **Release Announcements:**
   - Subscribe to the Go Announcements Mailing List to receive notifications about upcoming releases and security updates.

Keeping Your Codebase Current

1. **Test Against New Versions Early:**
   Before a major release, consider running your tests on the beta or release candidate. This helps identify any potential breaking changes and ensures a smoother upgrade process.

2. **Review Deprecation Warnings:**
   Check release notes for functions, packages, or language features that are being deprecated, and plan migrations accordingly.

3. **Leverage Go Modules:**
   Using Go modules (go mod) simplifies dependency management, making it easier to adopt newer versions of the Go standard library and third-party libraries.

Why Stay Updated?

1. **Improved Performance:**
   Each Go release often brings enhancements to the compiler, runtime, and garbage collector, resulting in faster builds and more efficient code execution.

2. **Access to New Features:**
   Features like generics, improved error handling, and new standard library packages are introduced in newer versions, enabling developers to write more concise and expressive code.

3. **Better Security:**
   Keeping your Go environment current ensures that known security vulnerabilities are patched, protecting your applications from potential threats.

11.4 Recommended Blogs, Podcasts, and Conferences

Beyond release notes and official documentation, the Go community offers a wealth of resources to help you stay informed, learn best practices, and keep improving your skills.

Blogs and Newsletters

1. **Go Blog (blog.golang.org):**
   The official blog is the primary source for announcements, new features, and technical deep dives.
2. **Go Weekly (golangweekly.com):**
   A curated newsletter that highlights recent blog posts, tutorials, open-source projects, and upcoming events.
3. **Dave Cheney's Blog (dave.cheney.net):**
   Offers practical advice, insights into Go performance, and reflections on language design.
4. **Cloud Native Go (medium.com/cloud-native-go):**
   Focused on building scalable and cloud-native applications in Go, covering tools, patterns, and best practices.

Podcasts

1. **Go Time (Changelog Media):**
   A weekly podcast featuring discussions with industry experts, covering Go news, libraries, frameworks, and development trends.
2. **GoTLDR:**
   Short, digestible episodes that summarize the latest Go news, releases, and tools.

3. **Ardan Labs Podcast:**

   Hosted by Bill Kennedy and the Ardan Labs team, offering in-depth interviews and technical topics.

Conferences and Meetups

1. **GopherCon:**

   The flagship Go conference held annually in the United States. Known for its high-quality talks, workshops, and networking opportunities.

2. **GopherCon Europe:**

   A Europe-based Go conference that brings together the international Go community.

3. **GoLab and Ardan Labs Events:**

   Regular workshops, training sessions, and smaller conferences focused on professional Go development.

4. **Local Meetups:**

   Many cities host Go meetups, which are great for connecting with other developers, sharing knowledge, and discussing new developments in the language.

Community Platforms

1. **Gopher Slack (invite at gophers.slack.com):**

   Join channels for announcements, libraries, job postings, and general discussions.

2. **Go Forum (forum.golangbridge.org):**

   An online forum where developers ask questions, share resources, and discuss Go projects.

3. **Reddit's Go Subreddit (r/golang):**

   A community-driven space to post news, tutorials, and open-source projects.

Staying Informed

By regularly checking these blogs, tuning into podcasts, attending conferences, and participating in the Go community, you'll be better equipped to:

- **Learn new techniques and patterns.**
- **Keep up with language changes and emerging tools.**
- **Build higher-quality, maintainable Go code.**

Being connected to the wider Go ecosystem ensures that you remain a knowledgeable and skilled Go developer.

Appendix

The appendix serves as a handy resource for quickly recalling Go syntax, referencing commonly used standard library packages, and understanding key idioms and terminology. It's meant to help both new and experienced developers navigate Go's ecosystem more efficiently.

A.1: Quick Reference for Go Syntax

1. Declaring Variables and Constants

go

Copy

```go
var x int      // zero-initialized to 0
var y = 42     // inferred type int
z := 100       // shorthand declaration and initialization
const pi = 3.14 // constant, must have a value
```

2. Functions

go

Copy

```go
// Basic function
func add(a int, b int) int {
    return a + b
}

// Multiple return values
func divide(a, b int) (quotient, remainder int) {
```

288

```go
    return a / b, a % b
}
```

3. Control Structures

go
Copy
```go
// If-else
if x > 10 {
    // do something
} else {
    // do something else
}

// For loop
for i := 0; i < 5; i++ {
    // iteration
}

// Range loop
nums := []int{1, 2, 3}
for index, value := range nums {
    // loop over slice
}

// Switch
switch x {
case 1:
    // case 1
case 2:
```

```go
    // case 2
default:
    // default case
}
```

4. Structs and Methods

```go
// Defining a struct
type Point struct {
    X, Y int
}

// Method associated with a struct
func (p Point) Distance() int {
    return p.X*p.X + p.Y*p.Y
}

// Pointer receiver for modifying the struct
func (p *Point) Move(dx, dy int) {
    p.X += dx
    p.Y += dy
}
```

5. Interfaces

```go
// Defining an interface
```

290

```go
type Shape interface {
    Area() float64
}

// Implementing an interface
type Circle struct {
    Radius float64
}

func (c Circle) Area() float64 {
    return 3.14 * c.Radius * c.Radius
}
```

6. Goroutines and Channels

go
Copy
```go
// Goroutine
go func() {
    // background task
}()

// Channel
ch := make(chan int)
go func() {
    ch <- 42
}()
val := <-ch
```

7. Error Handling

go

Copy

```go
func divide(a, b int) (int, error) {
    if b == 0 {
        return 0, fmt.Errorf("cannot divide by zero")
    }
    return a / b, nil
}
```

8. Defer, Panic, and Recover

go

Copy

```go
// Defer
func closeFile(file *os.File) {
    defer file.Close()
    // other operations
}

// Panic and Recover
func safeFunction() {
    defer func() {
        if r := recover(); r != nil {
            fmt.Println("Recovered from panic:", r)
        }
    }()
    panic("something went wrong")
}
```

292

A.2: Go Standard Library Cheat Sheet

1. Commonly Used Packages

fmt: For formatted I/O.

go
Copy

```
fmt.Println("Hello, World")
```

- **math:** Provides mathematical functions and constants.

  go
  Copy

  ```
  result := math.Sqrt(16)
  ```

- **net/http:** For building HTTP servers and clients.

  go
  Copy

  ```
  http.HandleFunc("/", func(w http.ResponseWriter, r *http.Request) {

  w.Write([]byte("Hello, World"))
  })
  http.ListenAndServe(":8080", nil)
  ```

- **os:** Handles operating system functions (files, environment variables).

  go
  Copy

  ```
  f, err := os.Open("file.txt")

  defer f.Close()
  ```

293

- **strings:** Provides string manipulation functions.

go

Copy

```
result := strings.ToUpper("hello")
```

- **time:** Deals with time-related functionality.

go

Copy

```
now := time.Now()
```

- **io and io/ioutil:** For input/output operations.

go

Copy

```
content, err := ioutil.ReadFile("file.txt")
```

2. Error Handling Helpers

errors: For creating simple error values.

go

Copy

```
err := errors.New("an error occurred")
```

- **fmt.Errorf:** For creating formatted error messages.

go

Copy

```
err := fmt.Errorf("error: %s", "something went wrong")
```

3. Synchronization and Concurrency

sync: Provides primitives like Mutex, WaitGroup.

go

Copy

```
var wg sync.WaitGroup
```

294

```
wg.Add(1)
go func() {
    // some concurrent work
    wg.Done()
}()
wg.Wait()
```

- **time:** For delays, timeouts, and periodic tasks.

go

Copy

```
time.Sleep(2 * time.Second)
```

4. JSON Handling

encoding/json:

go

Copy

```
var data map[string]interface{}
json.Unmarshal([]byte(`{"key": "value"}`), &data)
```

5. Command-Line Parsing

flag:

go

Copy

```
name := flag.String("name", "World", "a name to say hello to")
flag.Parse()
```

A.3: Glossary of Go Idioms and Terminology

- **Zero Value:**

    The default value assigned to a variable when no explicit initialization is provided. For example, 0 for integers, false for booleans, and nil for pointers, slices, and maps.

- **Go Routine:**

  A lightweight thread of execution managed by the Go runtime. Use go keyword to start a goroutine.

- **Channel:**

  A conduit through which goroutines communicate by sending and receiving values. Channels are typed and allow synchronization and data sharing.

- **Deferred Function Call:**

  A function call that is executed at the end of the containing function's scope. Often used for cleanup tasks like closing files or releasing locks.

- **Interface:**

  A type that defines a set of method signatures. Types that implement those methods are said to "satisfy" the interface. Interfaces enable polymorphism and decoupled code.

Type Assertion:

A way to extract a concrete type from an interface.

go

Copy

```
var i interface{} = 42
v, ok := i.(int)
```

- **Escape Analysis:**

  The compiler's process of determining whether a variable can be safely allocated on the stack (faster) or must be allocated on the heap (slower, but necessary if the variable outlives the function call).

Slicing a Slice:

Creating a new slice from a portion of an existing one.

go

Copy
```
s := []int{1, 2, 3, 4}
sub := s[1:3] // sub is [2, 3]
```

- **Embedded Types:**

  Including one struct or interface within another to promote its fields or methods.

  go

  Copy
```
type Base struct {
    ID int
}
type Derived struct {
    Base
    Name string
}
```

This quick reference, cheat sheet, and glossary aim to serve as a compact but comprehensive resource, helping you quickly recall Go syntax, find standard library solutions, and understand commonly used terminology.